"Leslie Davenport has trained many health professionals to be able to offer guided imagery to hospitalized patients. Through this groundbreaking leadership, she has inspired and witnessed many deeply moving and important moments in the lives of people facing serious health situations. She is a moving storyteller whose deeply spiritual approach is balanced by her sense of pragmatism and humor."

MARTIN L. ROSSMAN, MD,
author of *Fighting Cancer from Within*

"Leslie Davenport is an inspiring therapist and healer with a depth to her work that makes her an alchemist of the heart. She has a way of accompanying patients through the challenges of life-threatening illness, which leads them through unexpected portals to the joy of being fully human. A true pioneer in the field of integrative medicine, she brings a compassionate presence to her work, which elicits both clarity and insight that lead to true transformation."

DENNIS KENNY, D MIN, M DIV,
author of *Promise of the Soul*

"Leslie Davenport's personal spiritual journey has given her profound insights into the secret wisdom of the heart; her many years of healing work have given her the ability to help uncover that wisdom in others. Read these stories and see deep within yourself!"

STEVE BRATMAN, MD,
author of *The Natural Health Bible*

"Like icebergs floating in the sea—only partially visible to others and ourselves—a good part of what goes on in us lies beneath awareness. It helps to connect with the deep layer of fears and desires that shape us. Not to shed light where darkness is appropriate, but to glimpse the forces that make us who we are. When they are handled carefully, images span the gap between the dark unknown and the concerns of living. The bridge, the dialogue, and the connection are all healing. This book can help you make those connections, offering relief from the stresses and conflicts of living."

THOMAS MOORE,
author of *A Life at Work*

HEALING AND
TRANSFORMATION

THROUGH

SELF-GUIDED IMAGERY

Leslie Davenport

CELESTIAL ARTS
Berkeley | Toronto

Celestial Arts
an imprint of Ten Speed Press
PO Box 7123
Berkeley, CA 94707
www.tenspeed.com

Distributed in Australia by Simon and Schuster Australia, in Canada by Ten Speed Press
Canada, in New Zealand by Southern Publishers Group, in South Africa by Real Books, and
in the United Kingdom and Europe by Publishers Group UK.

Cover design and interior text design by Katy Brown

The excerpts from Alcoholics Anonymous are reprinted with permission of Alcoholics Anonymous World Services, Inc. (AAWS). Permission to reprint these excerpts does not mean that
AAWS has reviewed or approved the contents of this publication, or that AAWS necessarily
agrees with the views expressed herein. AA is a program of recovery from alcoholism only—
use of these excerpts in connection with programs and activities that are patterned after AA,
but which address other problems, or in any other non–AA context, does not imply otherwise.

The excerpted lines on page 7 from *Stray Birds* by Rabindranath Tagore, 1916, are reprinted
with permission of Forgotten Press, Mumbai, 2007.

"There Are Two Kinds if Intelligence" by Jalal ad-Din Rumi from *A Year with Rumi* by Coleman Barks. Copyright © 2006 by Coleman Barks. Reprinted by permission of HarperCollins
Publishers.

"Come, Come, Whoever You Are!" by Jalal ad-Din Rumi from *The Illuminated Rumi* translated
by Coleman Barks with illustrations by Michael Green. Copyright © 1997 by Coleman Barks
and Michael Green. Used by permission of Broadway Books, a division of Random House, Inc.

Library of Congress Cataloging-in-Publication Data

Davenport, Leslie.
    Healing and transformation through self-guided imagery / Leslie
Davenport.
        p. cm.
    Includes bibliographical references and index.
    ISBN 1-58761-324-7 (978-1-58761-324-1 : alk. paper) 1. Imagery
        (Psychology—Therapeutic use. I. Title.
    RC489.F35D38 2009
    616.89'14—dc22

                        2008005637

First printing, 2009
Printed in the United States of America
1 2 3 4 5 6 7 8 9 10 — 13 12 11 10 09

For my sons, Andrew and Ben,

who, forever and always,

keep my heart beaming.

Contents

Acknowledgments

I AM FORTUNATE to have a stellar team of professionals with me on this book. Special thanks go to my editor, Veronica Randall, to designer Katy Brown, and to former vice president Jo Ann Deck and former acquisitions manager Julie Bennett, four amazing women at Ten Speed Press whose creativity make my jaw drop. Thanks also to Jack Scovil, my literary agent, who is a wonderful advocate and champion.

I want to express my gratitude for the community that formed around me in the creation of this book. First, to my family—Mom, Jean, Dad, Tom (he cheers from the heavens along with sweet and sassy niece, Courtney), Andrew, Ben and Kendall, Kerry and John, Nancy and Jay—plus many friends and colleagues, whose gifts are woven into these pages. Some brought insight to the manuscript. Others bolstered my spirits and joined their enthusiasm with mine. To all of you who have offered your time, talents, and loving support, I give you my deep thanks.

I cannot count the many mentors and colleagues who have influenced me and so influenced this book. Although my first imagery teaching came through the lineage of Chishti Sufis and years of embodying living images in a dance career, I have also been influenced by Jeanne Achterberg; Academy of Guided Imagery founders Martin Rossman, MD, and David Bressler; Belleruth Naparstek; and spiritual teachers, including Thich Nhat Hanh, Byron Katie, and Eckhart Tolle.

And then there are my heart teachers, the many clients who have so openly shared the pain, beauty, confusion, and clarity of their lives. Some who share their stories are deeply disguised. Others have generously given permission to tell their stories without alterations or only thinly veiled. Special thanks go to the beautiful women in the wellness group, whose stories deserve a book of their own.

And infinite gratitude to the One glorious and mysterious Heart that so generously embraces us all.

Foreword

WE ALL HAVE DREAMS—night dreams, daydreams, and visions-yet-to-be-revealed. In our dreams and our own moments of worry and fantasy, each of us has extensive experience with the natural and powerful modes of imagery and visualization. Leslie Davenport has braided her experience and expertise in psychology, spiritual practices, and expressive arts with guided imagery. She has fashioned a practical approach to the healing aspects of imagery in ways that are understandable to all readers and useful in our daily lives.

Healing and Transformation through Self-Guided Imagery is an accessible guide to harnessing the power of our intuition and imagination. Leslie first brought this ancient practice to the halls of contemporary medicine eighteen years ago. Guided imagery is not limited to health crises, but while working with Leslie, I have seen the ways this powerful practice has benefited people in the hospital environment. Leslie is a true pioneer in bringing guided imagery into the mainstream of the practice of medicine.

We all respond to and tell others and ourselves stories as we share our images of the world. We are, in fact, all image makers and storytellers. Can we be open to the images that can support us in being the people we really are and living the lives we choose to live? Are we ready to begin a journey to the wisdom of our hearts? Leslie Davenport provides us a pathway to this healing wisdom.

William B. Stewart, MD
Institute for Health & Healing, California Pacific Medical Center
San Francisco, California

How Will This Book Be Useful to You?

*We know the truth not only
by reason, but by heart.*

BLAISE PASCAL

THIS BOOK IS A GUIDE to listening to your own heart. Every human heart is connected to a source of wisdom greater than our minds can understand. *Healing and Transformation through Self-Guided Imagery* shows you exactly how to tap into this source of wise advice by using guided imagery. Guided imagery is a natural, meditative process that reliably offers you direct access to you heart's wise guidance. Even your most painful and difficult experiences can be transformed, giving you a way to live with greater ease and joy.

Although the book delves into how and why imagery is effective, you do not need to read about imagery before you start using it in your own life. You can bring any concern directly to the Self-Facilitation Worksheet in Chapter 4, which takes you to your heart's guidance in a six-step process. Applicable to every situation, it offers detailed instructions you can use by yourself or with a partner to awaken your inner senses, discover your inner sanctuary, and receive your heart's message for your particular issue. The chapters that follow Chapter 4 address the questions that most often arise when people begin to use imagery, and provide even more ways to access inner wisdom.

Having established guided imagery programs in five hospitals since 1989, as well as offering it within my private practice, I have personally witnessed the rewards of this work in thousands of lives. So often, I join dynamic, productive people at a point when life has pulled the rug out from under their feet through an unanticipated crisis and they find themselves flat on their backs. I have seen how consistently imagery offers a way not simply to help us get back on our feet, but also to help us stand up in our lives with even greater wisdom and fulfillment than before. I find great joy in writing this hands-on book to make the power of guided imagery directly available to everyone.

Through the personal stories of both clients and self-facilitators found in each chapter, you can peer into the tender hearts of eleven people who brought their crises to a guided imagery process. These stories illustrate the powerful healing available in the approach you will be learning.

The stories focus on moments of radical transformation elicited through guided imagery. Some of the people you will read about have been moving for quite some time toward a new understanding about themselves and life. Then we see the moment when, like fruit ripening on a branch, they effortlessly drop into new perspectives. Others seem to discover their inner wisdom as quickly and unexpectedly as they found themselves in the original crisis. These surprisingly quick insights are possible because guided imagery brings us to the truly amazing inner wisdom that is always available within. Most of us just don't turn toward our heart's wisdom regularly or haven't quite known how to do so.

You will witness for yourself how crisis can be the catalyst for peace that can emerge from behind a fortress of emotional pain. You will see how others call forth their heart's wisdom as a guide through cancer treatment, marital crisis, the loss of their home, and financial trouble, to name just a few examples. Perhaps you will recognize a path out of your own stress.

If you are currently facing one of these challenges, you may wish to jump ahead to these real-life stories. In addition to using the worksheet for practical insights into your own situation, you can also use the unique Eyes Open Imagery process, which follows each story, to deepen your understanding.

Life is rich with imagery, whether our eyes are closed or open. This book shows you not only a reliable path into your deep, inner wisdom but also teaches you how to open your spiritual eyes in daily life, allowing you to recognize messages from the heart of the world. You will see how the mystery and sacred gift of life are here right now, even in simple things like the ability to read these little dabs of black ink on paper and communicate. How remarkable that is!

Eyes Open Imagery is an invaluable bridge between our inner and outer worlds, bringing all our perceptions to life. There are Eyes Open Imagery exercises following each of the stories of transformation. Even if you are not dealing with the specific concern illustrated in the story, the benefits of the practices reach far beyond any particular theme. I invite you to try these practices and discover with fresh eyes the rich universe within and around you.

Using imagery as a self-help tool when facing a major life stressor is only the beginning of tapping into the potential of this powerful practice. Imagery is far more than self-help; it can be a way to self-realization. By regularly traveling to our heart's domain, we not only get in touch with, but also become at home in, a source of wisdom greater than we know. Using imagery this way can uproot underlying beliefs that promote distress in our lives. Often, intuition naturally emerges in day-to-day awareness as we cultivate receptivity to our inner guidance. Over time, you may find that situations that previously would have been upsetting to you are now no longer disturbing.

Healing and Transformation through Self-Guided Imagery

Imagery is a wonderful companion to other meditative and growth approaches. Chapter 11 will show you specific ways to weave together guided imagery with other types of inner work, using the examples of Byron Katie's inquiry method, cognitive-behavioral therapy, and twelve-step programs. Blending imagery with other methods has a synergistic effect, often increasing the benefits of each approach.

I hope you will also visit www.LeslieDavenport.com, where you will find free, downloadable guided imagery sessions that accompany many of the exercises in the book. You can also submit questions to support you in your practice.

There are many ways to use this book. I trust that your heart will show you the way that is exactly right for you.

There are two kinds of intelligence: one acquired,

As a child in school memorizes facts and concepts. . . .

There is another kind of tablet, one

Already completed and preserved inside you.

A spring overflowing its springbox.

A freshness in the center of the chest. . . .

JALAL AD-DIN RUMI

CHAPTER ONE

SEEING WITH THE EYES OF THE HEART

DEEP IN EVERY HEART lives a wellspring of wisdom. As practical as they are mysterious, our hearts can connect us to the essence of life itself. Our heart's wisdom comes to us as universal images and symbols, and it arises within all cultures and eras. In contemporary Western society, guided imagery is one of the ways to discover this natural, ancient source of wisdom within.

Guided imagery is a process that focuses our attention inward to receive the impressions, pictures, and dream figures arising from our true nature. These images are the natural expression of our intuition, unconscious mind, and deepest self. They hold the key to living a life of greater ease and fulfillment. Guided imagery gives us a way to receive our heart's wise advice, unmediated by the habitual thinking and limiting beliefs that drive the vast majority of our day-to-day experience. As we evoke this way of knowing, it can help us meet our greatest challenges.

Life is rich with imagery, whether your eyes are closed or open. You can call forth wisdom from the images that arise within your own heart, but you will also learn to receive guidance from the living images in the world around you. The process of receiving inner images will be referred to as guided imagery, and gleaning insight from the physical images expressed in the world will be explored through Eyes Open Imagery practices.

For example, as you learn guided imagery, you will see how a tree could appear as an inner symbol in a guided imagery session and offer insight for your life. What if the tree outside your window, a living image, has a message for you, too? As you cultivate the "eyes of the heart," you will experience directly how the rich images in the natural world are brimming with wisdom, ready to guide you as well.

We have all heard the adage that every crisis is an opportunity in disguise, and yet to truly live from this perspective is something very few of us achieve. Life is tremendously challenging. Buddhism goes so far as to say that one of the Four Noble Truths is that life *is* suffering. Most of us can relate. Although everyone acknowledges that life is change, we nevertheless resist it and feel resentful when change occurs. This is especially true when changes run contrary to our view of what we think should be happening.

Yet life has a pattern of pulling the rug out from under our feet. We envision a future of how, where, and with whom we are going to be happy. We set goals and apply efforts toward achieving these pictures of success. It seems we are happily on our way to this "ever after," when, suddenly, fate wraps its bony fingers around the edge of the carpet. We get fired from our job, or our partner leaves us. We become ill, or our home is damaged in a flood. Change often leaves us hurting and bewildered.

Psychology measures stress in terms of change. This scale includes life changes deemed negative, such as unexpectedly being laid off from a job, but it also rates stress from changes considered positive, such as a job promotion. Any shift of status quo, anticipated or surprising, creates stress along with the full array of physical and emotional symptoms. When stress is intense or prolonged, we easily feel overwhelmed and find ourselves in crisis. And here is a crucial key to understanding and transforming crisis: what turns unexpected life changes into suffering is our unexamined thinking. Our minds compulsively recycle distressing and unproductive thoughts. Guided imagery brings our painful thought patterns to light and guides us toward new perspectives waiting in the heart.

But there is more to this than just getting through a crisis and going back to normal. Rather than going back, there is a way to stand up and go forward with even greater strength and meaning than before. A catastrophe can truly become a sacred threshold if we know how to tap into our inner wisdom.

In the Chinese language, the logogram for "crisis" is comprised of two characters signifying "danger" and "opportunity." This Eastern symbol points to the invitation for transformation embedded within every crisis. This invitation can go unheard, unfelt, unrealized, and unnoticed in the noise of daily life, but guided imagery gives us reliable access to the potential opportunity of such moments.

The crux of this powerful shift comes when we move our focus from the pictures created by our thoughts about what should be happening and turn instead to the images arising from our heart. The poet John O'Donohue, in his book *Beauty: The Invisible Embrace*, describes it this way: "Somewhere in every heart there is a discerning voice. . . . It . . . opens up a new perspective through which the concealed meaning of a situation might emerge. . . . This faithful voice can illume the dark lands of despair. . . . This voice brings us directly into contact with the inalienable presence of beauty in the soul."

Roselyn, a petite and energetic woman in her early forties, is at such a turning point. Having recently undergone a lumpectomy for breast cancer, she is soon to begin radiation treatment. She came to my therapy practice to try guided imagery.

An advertising executive for a large corporation, Roselyn is adept at organizing and preparing for important events, and she tries to apply these skills to addressing her medical needs. She arrives at my office carrying a large leather briefcase full of carefully arranged files of her recent research on cancer and treatment options. She sifts through her notes and hands me three research articles on the benefits of guided imagery. She tells me in great detail how the lymphocytes and antibodies work in the bloodstream and describes the function of the helper T-cells and B-cells. It is clear that Roselyn has virtually scripted the scenario of what she believes to be the correct functioning of her immune system. Roselyn is motivated, prepared, and eager to communicate this script to her body. But what comes through the imagery, as her focus shifts from her thoughts to her heart, takes her completely by surprise.

As we begin our session, I invite Roselyn to close her eyes. With a breathing exercise and progressive relaxation, she gradually becomes deeply at ease. When her body and mind are quiet, I ask Roselyn to let an image form for her own well-functioning immune system.

"I'm about eleven, in the patio of my parent's home. It's early evening, a warm summer night, and I can smell the barbecued sausage that we just finished for dinner." With her eyes still closed, her brows pinched together, she looks both curious and awestruck. "Sheba, my tabby cat, is beginning to give birth to a litter of kittens. I feel panicky about what I should do to help her. My parents are down the street at a neighbor's house, and I'm by myself."

"What happens next?" I ask.

"I just stay by her side, and it feels like she really, really likes that. Oh! I can see that she knows exactly what to do." She pauses and tilts her head, squinting a little even though her eyes remain closed. A smile spreads across her face. I can only imagine the scene unfolding in her mind.

"The kittens are launched into the world perfect and healthy. She cleans them, nurtures them. It's simple, in a way, and so natural."

After the session, she lingers in the awe of witnessing birth. She speaks much more slowly now and looks directly into my eyes.

"I had it all wrong. Sheba didn't have to figure out how to give birth, and I don't need to figure out how to produce blood cells."

There is a pause while we both appreciate the beauty of this.

"But what I must do," she reaches for a tissue as tears well up, "is learn to be present to myself. The way I stood by Sheba."

Roselyn then describes the high-pressured, fast-paced lifestyle that has kept her out of touch with her body's natural rhythms. Coming from a work-hard/play-hard philosophy, she pushes herself into whatever is next, running on four or five hours of sleep, eating on the go, and keeping her energy up with coffee and sweets.

"I can see how I've mistreated my body. It's not even close to how I would care for a pet . . . or a friend. I've steamrolled it and taken it for granted. And I was going to steamroll my cancer treatment! I can't believe I hadn't realized this before."

Roselyn's profound realization about herself prompted a new direction in her lifestyle and priorities. This significant shift from believing we know what's best for us to a deeper understanding of our healing is central to what the guided imagery process reveals. So beautifully reliable, time and again, the insights from guided imagery erupt through our limiting, constructed beliefs. What had been hidden from Roselyn's awareness suddenly seemed obvious to her.

Over the next few weeks, our work together helped Roselyn expand her awareness of her body's needs and rhythms. She was learning to receive from within messages she had previously been filtering out. Her edge softened, and a sweetness emerged that had not been evident in our initial meeting. She was finally becoming a friend to herself.

When Roselyn had first come into my office, she believed that she had the necessary tools to approach her healing. She was ready to implement the same organized and effective method that served her so well in her career. Her concepts about imagery had even been confirmed through research conducted by experts in the field.

But the source of wisdom within cannot be found in any research article. What each person needs as he faces a challenging situation are images containing guidance that address the unique nature of his circumstances. And the imagery wellspring within, consistently comes forth in that immediate and unique way. Roselyn discovered wisdom she didn't even know she had.

Although later we did go on to have imagery sessions that included seeing and feeling the effective action of the cells in her immune system, this occurred in the context of a new, larger understanding. Roselyn's more comprehensive perspective could not have emerged if we had started out by sticking with her self-prescribed imagery agenda.

We could say that Roselyn's eyes became more open when they were closed. In other words, Roselyn discovered that she could actually see the wisdom she needed by looking with the eyes of her heart through guided imagery. In daily life, we could say our eyes are sometimes more closed when they are open. How many times have we missed really seeing a beautiful day when we walk down the street because our inner eyes are on a mental shopping list? We can also learn to see the world around us with the eyes of the heart through a new practice called Eyes Open Imagery.

Eyes Open Imagery invites us to receive the messages coming to us all the time from living images in the world. If in our daily lives we cultivate the same quality of openhearted receptivity used in guided imagery, then the heart of the world is revealed to us.

What would it take to see the world with the eyes of your heart? Carl Jung, in his book *Visions: Notes of the Seminar Given in 1930–1934*, describes the art of seeing this way: "[L]ooking, psychologically, brings about the activation of the object; it is as if something were emanating from our spiritual eye that evokes or activates the object of one's vision."

To see with *your* "spiritual eye" requires cultivating awareness by looking at things with fewer preconceived notions, having a calm presence, and being receptive to what is in front of *you*. In his poem *Stray Birds*, Bengali poet Rabindranath Tagore wrote,

Do not say, "it is morning,"
and dismiss it with a name of yesterday.
See it for the first time
as a newborn child that had no name.

Eyes Open Imagery allows us to perceive the world anew in its natural state of aliveness and wonder.

Thich Nhat Hanh, a Vietnamese Zen master, tells us in his book *The Sun My Heart: From Mindfulness to Insight Contemplation,* "You can disregard the idea that you must close your eyes to look inside and open them to look outside. . . . If you live in awareness, it is easy to see miracles everywhere."

Included in this book are thirty-three Eyes Open Imagery practices that teach you how to cultivate this kind of receptive awareness, three practices at the end of each personal story of healing and transformation. Even if you are not dealing with the specific concern illustrated in a particular story, the benefits of these practices reach far beyond the theme of any one story. Let's look at a few examples of how these Eyes Open Imagery exercises work.

Next, you will meet Evelyn, an elegant woman entering hospice care who realized through guided imagery that her grandson would be taken care of when she was no longer around to help him. She came to realize that life itself was already supporting him in a complete and perfect way.

In the Eyes Open Imagery exercises that accompany Evelyn's story, you can also experience firsthand, with your eyes open, how life is supporting you beautifully in a complete and perfect way.

The story of Daniel introduces you to a successful executive who, after suffering a heart attack, uncovered through guided imagery how he had been driven by an unconsciously held belief learned from his father, which he ultimately let go of in order to champion his own life dreams.

The Eyes Open Imagery exercises that come with Daniel's story show you how to bring your unexamined beliefs into the light of awareness and remove any of the old family messages that no longer serve you.

I invite you to keep an Eyes Open Imagery journal. Drawing or writing about the experiences that come from doing each exercise can help you anchor the insights in your life. Additional perspectives will also surface through the journaling process. Chronicling your experiences creates a rich treasury of your inner life that you can return to time and again to rekindle the experiences you have found most valuable.

But it is not enough to know that images from within and around us can mobilize our healing responses and communicate guidance. To make use of this valuable tool, we must first discover the gateway though which these images can be welcomed into our lives.

Evelyn:
End-of-Life Issues

To the mind that is still,
the whole universe surrenders.

LAO TZU

AN INDEPENDENT, educated woman, Evelyn expresses herself with a tough refinement, a Katharine Hepburn kind of elegance. There is a quiet power to her presence, unassuming, yet with a tangible authority that rises from her life experiences. She celebrates the subtle beauty in everyday moments that could easily be overlooked as simply mundane. I had worked with her briefly about a year earlier, and she had made a strong impression on me.

I rarely make house calls. For most psychotherapists, the therapeutic container of the office is a significant part of creating a clear arena for facilitating change. At eighty-seven, Evelyn has not been able to drive for several months's because of her declining eyesight. But I make an exception in response to Evelyn's request for an appointment at her house. I step into a home with muted colors and lighting, beautiful art that is sparsely distributed but intentionally placed. It feels so like Evelyn, and it evokes stillness in me.

Evelyn shares the characteristic of many in her generation of prefer-ing to keep the details of her medical situation a private matter. She does, however, share with me that she recently met with hospice on the advice of her physician. The stiffness in her walk and pinched brow tell me that she is in physical pain. We sit in her living room, and she props a cush-ion behind her back. Evelyn displays a transparency I have witnessed in many people toward the end of their lives. Blue rivers of veins are visible beneath sheer, papery skin. And at times, her spirit flares so brightly I lose track of what she is saying.

"I'm ready to go," she announces in a simple matter-of-fact way. "Somehow I knew how to be born, and I'm confident that I know how to leave." She calls for the appointment because she wants to resolve out-standing issues with her grown children and grandchildren. We explore together her close relationships. It is a grandson, age twenty-seven, who causes her distress. Something of the "lost child" in the family system, Matt has had past struggles with drugs and has not yet established a solid career direction or stable personal relationship. Evelyn has been a safe confidant for him, and she worries about the impact of her declin-ing availability to him. She knows she has been a source of strength and understanding that may have helped him stay out of trouble. We explore this concern through guided imagery.

Relaxed, with eyes closed, she begins describing the scene that emerges in her mind's eye. "I'm in a forest glen with deep shades of green. It's lush, carpeted with ferns, and full of filtered sunlight. The air is comfortably warm and very moist. It feels like late morning, maybe 11:00 or so. I'm resting on a fallen branch that makes a natural bench. I hear a stream somewhere nearby, the occasional sound of insects, and the rustling of small animals in the leaves. It feels feminine somehow, and safe. It's very nourishing."

I encourage her to take time and enjoy the nourishing qualities. We pause together in silence.

"Just breathing the air feels like food. The entire forest is breathing with me." The nourishment from this place seems to ease her pain and her body softens.

I ask her if this is a good place and time to focus on her grandson Matt. She agrees. "Allow an image to form for your relationship with Matt," I say. In response, she feels a pull to explore a path through the trees and see where it leads.

"I'm entering a clearing, and there are two trees in the opening. It's a large redwood and a young seedling." She focuses on the smaller tree. "This tree has had some branches broken off, and the trunk is a little crooked, but it's really vital, healthy." She senses the connection to Matt, and her smile shows a sense of relief. I invite her to say more about what brings a smile to her face.

"I know he's okay. I trust that." Her voice is clear and strong.

"What about the larger tree?" I inquire. Although nothing is visible in her demeanor, I feel her internal eyes moving to the other tree. This subtle attunement to Evelyn's internal state feels similar to the experience of feeling someone's eyes on the back of my head before turning to look behind me.

"There is a majestic presence," she pauses before continuing, "a deep silence coming from the redwood." Her voice sounds deeper, more resonant, as she speaks.

I encourage her to get acquainted with this powerful tree. "What else do you notice about this tree?" I ask.

"The tree is female, and she instructs me to look around at the field and forest. The message is something like, 'Look how things are being tended.' It reminds me of a scriptural passage I haven't thought about in years but I've always loved: 'Consider the lilies of the fields, how they grow; they toil not, neither do they spin: And yet I say unto you that even Solomon in all his glory was not arrayed like one of these.'"

Somehow her face looks more radiant, as though the sunlight from this meadow were seeping though her skin.

She continues, "The redwood is telling me that nature is the gardener. The trees have what they need—sunlight, water, earth, and air—to thrive. The support for life and growth is abundant. There is no lack of what's needed. No tree or plant relies on another completely or on an isolated element. The nourishment flows in from everywhere."

There are rich, long pauses between the sentences, a slow rhythm with these images and messages. As a way of integrating these images with her initial question, I ask her to tell me whether this place seems related to her concerns about Matt.

"Oh, yes," she replies. "It's a message that Matt is taken care of. How can he not be, with the friends, family, and unexpected gifts from life he will discover? There is a natural cycle of things that come and go. Perhaps my departure will open new possibilities for him that would not be available otherwise. It has been wonderful to grow near each other, but he doesn't need me." She speaks this perspective without any sense of personal diminishment. There is no devaluing of the special relationship the two of them have enjoyed, just a simple acknowledgement that the understanding of how life goes on is so much bigger than she had considered.

"There's so much life here," she continues. She takes in long slow breaths, as if breathing in that nourishment again. "And death, too. If I really look, I see that there are leaves turning brown and dry, and new buds forming, and fully matured plants in the height of their life cycle. It is all so beautiful—the bud, the flower, the bare branch."

I ask Evelyn if there is anything else wanting to be explored in the imagery, and she lets me know it feels complete. As we come out of the session, a sense of peace surrounds Evelyn. She also looks tired.

She closes her eyes for a moment and somehow she looks astonishingly beautiful to me. There is an expansive feeling in my chest that often arises when I see a particularly glorious sunset.

Most seasoned hospital nurses would affirm the old adage that people die the way they live. If they have been fighters in life, they often

Healing and Transformation through Self-Guided Imagery

push back on the dying process. A person who has cultivated acceptance brings that quality into the last phase of living. It will not surprise me if Evelyn's wish to release her body with simple surrender and natural timing came to pass.

We sit for a few more moments, comfortable in the quiet house. The sunlight seems brighter in the patches on the carpet, and we hear the breeze in the leaves outside the window. I gather my things, and we walk slowly toward the front door. On the dining table are several peonies beginning to fade, with some stems folded at odd angles in the vase and a few petals scattered on the tabletop.

As if on cue, one more petal falls off the stem.

She turns to me, her eyes bright, and whispers, "That's how I want to go."

EYES OPEN IMAGERY:
Cultivating an Awareness That Life Supports You

- Find an outdoor setting where you can view people, plants, and buildings. Locate a plant at the beginning of its life cycle, perhaps a seedling or bud. Then find a plant in full bloom. Where can you see a plant at the end of its life? Notice the relationship of these different cycles of life: Are there dry leaves at the base of the plant that are now becoming mulch? Is there a new plant sprouting out of a seed from last season's flower?

  Imagine a fast-forward film clip of the scene in front of you spanning ten years. Watch the people come and go; see the plants rise, blossom, and fade with the seasons; you might even watch an old building crumble and be replaced. If this landscape, this living image, had a voice, what would it be expressing to you?

- Take some time outside to really look at the blossom of a single flower. Notice the form, colors, shape, texture, and aroma. Realize that the water in the petals was once rain, the strength of the stem has shaped itself from the rich nutrients of the earth, and the vibrancy began as sunlight. Now sense the vitality, the glow, the aliveness that animates the flower. What does this flower want you to know?

- You can also do the same exercise looking at your hand. Really notice the colors, shape, texture, and scent. See your hand as if for the very first time. Remember the food from the earth you have eaten that has now become your body. Realize the elements of water, air, earth, and sun that became the food. Then sense the vitality, the glow, the aliveness that animate your body. Close your eyes and feel that aliveness throughout and around you. If this aliveness had a voice, what would it want you to know?

CHAPTER TWO

THE THRESHOLD
OF IMAGERY

In the beginning . . . the earth was without form.

GENESIS

THE GUIDED IMAGERY PROCESS clears the way for spontaneous, joyful living. Guided imagery connects us to our internal environment, inviting us to trust our intuition and creativity and to reside in
our vibrant, core self.

But where do these images come from? And where is the doorway to access images? Images meet us in *liminal* space. Liminal comes
from the Latin word for "threshold." Liminality is entered as we exit
the terrain of the old, but when the new is not yet formed. As we witnessed with Roselyn, letting go of her expectations about imagery and
her belief in the "right" way to engage her immune system allowed her
to enter a clear space where meaningful and unforeseen images could
emerge. She was in a place of unknowing, and it is exactly that lack of
certainty that allowed the images to arise that spoke directly to her
immediate concerns.

Anthropologist Victor Turner, in his book *The Ritual Process: Structure and Anti-Structure,* made a significant contribution to the understanding of liminal space in his work with the Ndembu tribe of central Africa

in the 1950s. Turner recorded rituals wherein boys of the tribe became men. Observing these rites of passage, he witnessed how entering an experience outside of our known identity can create a potent limbo that enables transformation to take place. To cross the gap between stages of life, the pubescent males were separated from both the children and the men. They were temporarily stripped of a role that defined a place of belonging within the tribe. This twilight passage became a place of waiting, of listening, of ambiguity and incubation. The passage gradually evolved into a birth canal that reshaped a new identity. But this betwixt-and-between phase is not limited to formal rituals, and it shows up in a wide variety of ways throughout our lives.

A liminal space opens during a radical transition: between relationships, between jobs, between homes, or with the change in our health that accompanies a life-threatening diagnosis, to give just a few examples. Any time we turn a corner and there's no going back, we are on liminal ground. Often these transitions touch us deeply, changing not only our life circumstances, but also altering our sense of self.

Being out of the familiar and facing the unknown can be terrifying. Richard Rohr, Franciscan priest and author, in his article published in the *National Catholic Reporter*, "Days without Answer in a Narrow Space—Lent," describes well how difficult it can be to inhabit liminal space. "If we are security-needy by temperament, we will always run back to the old room that we have already constructed. If we are risk-taking by temperament, we will quickly run to a new one of our own making and liking. Hardly anyone wants to stay on the threshold without knowing the answers."

As unsettling as these radical transitions can be, they are ultimately unavoidable. It becomes more a question of how we will relate to them. Although difficult and often painful, they also yield some of the greatest gifts in the unfolding of our lives. By their very nature, radical transitions evoke questions of the soul.

Healing and Transformation through Self-Guided Imagery

Crossing over a threshold where things can no longer be the same calls forth the soul's invitation to cast off old patterns that no longer serve. Like a snake that literally outgrows its own skin, the call to shed old strategies and limiting viewpoints lets us expand into a new mode of being. We discover ways to stand in our life that bring even greater integrity to what we truly value. We can embrace the opportunity to come home to ourselves.

That which we find comfortable and familiar we can mistake for wisdom. We like to be right, and it feels good to believe that we know what to do. We all develop constellations of beliefs that become lenses through which we perceive the world. Most of us are unaware of these filters. It's like forgetting that we are wearing glasses that bring a certain field of vision into focus.

For example, a child raised in a chaotic home with an alcoholic parent can develop the belief that speaking up for yourself is dangerous. When the child leaves home as an adult, he or she typically will continue to peer through this same lens in all relationships both personal and professional. For someone with this family background, challenging a work policy, for example, would automatically be seen as too threatening to voice, even when the suggestion might actually be welcomed. Henry M. Tomlinson says it beautifully in his book *Out of Soundings*: "We do not see things as they are, but as we ourselves are."

We must risk facing the unknown and move willingly into mystery to discover which truths have staying power. We must move beyond our ideas about life to receive its ultimate fullness. It is a powerful and liberating experience when we see old lenses for what they are and remove them with guided imagery.

With guided imagery, this liminal space can be approached intentionally, whether or not our life circumstances are undergoing dramatic change. Any time we choose to welcome it, the guided imagery process provides a doorway through which we can receive wisdom from our inner world. Science has estimated that conscious thought uses only about 10 percent of our mental capacity. This leaves vast reservoirs of consciousness untouched. Across the threshold of liminal space, guided imagery shines a spotlight into untapped inner dimensions.

So how do we get to liminal space and the images that arise within it? The great theologian Meister Eckhart is translated by James Clark and John Skinner in *Meister Eckhart: Selected Treatises and Sermons* as saying, "God is not attained by a process of addition to anything in the soul, but by a process of subtraction." The same is true of liminal space. Liminal space is the openness behind our mental chatter. When we "subtract" our mental chatter, we have liminal space. Like the sun that is always present even when hidden behind clouds, liminal space is always available, and we enter it when our habitual thought patterns dissipate.

Many spiritual practices exist for the purpose of entering liminal space. One example is found in Zen Buddhism—the practice of *shoshin*, or "beginner's mind." This approach challenges the practitioner to release any claims of mastery on areas of knowledge, regardless of how long or how deeply they have been studying. Zen priest and author Shunryu Suzuki begins his book, *Zen Mind, Beginner's Mind*, with a quotation that points to the tremendous potential of this type of awareness when he states, "In the beginner's mind there are many possibilities. In the expert's mind there are few." Letting go of what we think we know enables the liminal to be entered and wisdom of the heart to arise naturally.

The rhythms of nature can also point us to the threshold of liminal space. Nature's pulse is an ebb and flow that can be seen in the movement of the tides, the turning of the seasons, the rising and setting of the sun. In quantum physics, subatomic particles are believed to blink on and off. On the grandest scale, the cosmos pulsates in expansion and contraction.

The transition points between pulses are liminal. Transitions create a momentary pause, a suspension: the wave breaking on shore just before it is pulled back into the sea, the barren winter branches before

Healing and Transformation through Self-Guided Imagery

the spring buds burst forth. Or consider the familiar lull that accompanies dawn or dusk. Everything quiets in that transitional time. Benedictine monk Bede Griffiths relates his experience in his autobiography *The Golden String*: "Everything then grew still as the sunset faded and the veil of dusk began to cover the earth . . . and in the hush that comes before sunset, I felt again the presence of an unfathomable mystery."

Our own breathing is an example of this natural ebb and flow. Take a moment now and bring your attention to your breathing. Without changing your breath pattern, notice that there is a natural pause at the end of each exhalation prior to the next in-breath. There is the suspension, the window into stillness. Liminal space is found in the silence before and after sound, the spaciousness surrounding structure, and the still point within movement.

Liminal space is perhaps more familiar to those in the arts, for what can seem like an empty void is actually the birthplace of creativity itself. Emptiness can be as fertile and mysterious as a womb.

When a composer writes those first notes of a melody that have never existed before, inspiration becomes sound. The painter facing a blank canvas brushes colors into a reality never seen before that moment. The spin and leap of the choreographer on an open stage is the creative impulse finding form moment by moment.

Manifestation occurs when an inspiration, quality, or impulse arises as an ethereal impression from liminal space and crosses the threshold into shapes, colors, textures, movements, sounds, and so on. John Bennett, who studied sacred dance with the Armenian mystic G. I. Gurdjieff, describes in the *Sevenfold Work* the state of mind that accompanies standing on the creative threshold. "We allow the movement to do itself. . . . In this condition it is difficult to describe our state of consciousness. It can be said that we are both lucidly aware of everything that is happening and also conscious of nothing. We lose hold on our ordinary kind of self-awareness. . . . It is when it no longer comes out of our own cleverness and powers. This is the essence of the art that is significant, which helps to change or enrich the world and bewilders the artist himself if he does not come to understand how the reality must come through him and not by him."

These creative realms are not a domain exclusive to the artist, and you will experience them. Through guided imagery we encounter shapes, colors, textures, movements, and sounds in liminal space, arising out of our own heart. In fact, internal images have accompanied humanity in every culture and in all human endeavors. In Chapter 3 you will see how the historical roots of guided imagery were an essential part of Egyptian and hermetic philosophy. We will trace its appearance through a variety of spiritual traditions such as tantric yoga, shamanism, and early contemplative Christianity. And we will discover ways that guided imagery is an integral part of contemporary life, including imagery's contribution to psychology, sports performance, medicine, and even quantum physics.

AUDREY:
SPIRITUAL HEARTACHE

Light (God's eldest daughter!)

THOMAS FULLER

AUDREY HAS A GOOD LIFE, a very good life. She meditates regularly and has actively been in some form of spiritual exploration for the past fifteen years. In her early forties, she's energetic and trim, partly due to her rigorous yoga practice. She's attentive to diet, using organic products whenever possible. She gets satisfaction and meaning from running a nonprofit for disadvantaged children and is thankful for the good service the organization is providing to the community. Although not currently in a relationship, she has a close circle of friends and a rich social life. She has a cute apartment and is ready to buy a house in the next couple of years. Her life is going extremely well. She just doesn't know why her heart bears a deep, consuming ache.

"Does everyone feel this way? Am I in an existential crisis? Am I lonely and just don't realize it? Do I need to see a cardiologist, a psychiatrist? Am I just too sensitive or self-absorbed? Do I have hormone problems?"

Audrey will sincerely tell you that she's happy—mostly, content. And being with her, it does seem to be true. But in the quiet moments, the exquisitely private moments, she feels her biting heartache, often accompanied by tears that seem to flow from a bottomless well, and she can't figure out why.

She lights a candle, as she often does to open her meditation practice, and begins an imagery journey on heartache.

Journey to the Wisdom of the Heart
SELF-FACILITATION WORKSHEET

1. WHAT DO YOU NEED GUIDANCE ABOUT? (ONE MINUTE)

Write one word or phrase to stand for the topic on which you wish to receive inner guidance from your heart. Make it as short as possible. For example, if your concern is "My ex-husband is late again with a child-support payment. He breaks his agreements time and again. What shall I do?" you would write "my ex" or "finances," depending on which is closest to your real concern.

Write the word or phrase on the piece of paper. Turn the paper over and set it aside, trusting that in just a few minutes, a greater wisdom than you now possess will fully address your concern.

Audrey's Topic: *Heartache*

2. JOURNEY TO YOUR HEART BY TRAVELING INWARD (THREE TO FOUR MINUTES)

The journey to your heart begins as soon as you close your eyes. Bring your attention to your breathing. Each time you breathe in, silently say the word *clarity*. Every time you exhale, silently say the word *peace* and feel your body relaxing. Any time you find your thoughts wandering, bring your focus back to your breath and relax-

Healing and Transformation through Self-Guided Imagery

ation. Continue for about three minutes, until you are as relaxed as possible.

Audrey's Journey: *As soon as I close my eyes, the familiar tears start. It feels like someone has placed one of those lead X-ray vests from the dentist's office on my chest. It's very intense, very heavy. I just breathe, staying present to the physical intensity, so similar to being with strong body sensations in my yoga practice. I don't try to change anything, but just relax with whatever is happening. It lightens slightly as I breathe. I sit quietly.*

3. DISCOVERING YOUR INNER SANCTUARY (THREE MINUTES)

Now that you're relaxed, imagine a place where you can feel even more peaceful. It may be a beach, a meadow, or a quiet room in your home. It could even be an imaginary place. Whatever appears, let it be a setting where you can be completely yourself, free from pressures or expectations. Where you find yourself may surprise you, but let your heart show you where it wants to meet you. Even if you have done this process before, you may find yourself in a new environment that is just right for today. Whether you find yourself indoors or outdoors, settle into the most comfortable spot and enjoy the colors, sounds, scents, and feel of this safe and special place.

Audrey's Inner Sanctuary: *It's as if I'm the size of a bee. I'm lying back in a rose blossom, surrounded by fleshy, pink walls of moist petals. There are smaller rose petals being pressed gently on my face and arms (I don't know who is doing that, but I don't care!). The moisture and very faint rose scent feels like a healing balm. It's like I'm eating light—or my skin is absorbing the light of the petals. I'm resting so softly. It feels like nature's womb. I can see the diffuse light of the sun glowing softly through the walls of petals.*

4. BRINGING YOUR TOPIC TO HEART (ONE MINUTE)

Now imagine your paper being delivered to you in this wonderful place. In your mind's eye, view your concern again. Feel your distress embraced by the qualities of your inner sanctuary. Imagine holding your paper and concern lightly in your upturned palms and know that you are about to receive clear guidance from your heart.

Audrey's Topic: *Heartache*

5. RECEIVING YOUR HEART'S MESSAGE (THREE TO FIVE MINUTES)

In your sanctuary, ask your heart for a wise and loving response to your issue. Let your heart's reply appear as an image a few feet in front of you. Whatever symbol appears, receive it as an honored guest. Whether it is a color, a figure, a phrase, or an impression, notice its texture, shape, sound, and so on. Feel the qualities that this image embodies. What does it want you to know about your concern? How do you feel in the presence of your heart's wise advice?

Audrey's Heart's Message: *I ask my heart, "Please help me understand my heartache." A lit candle appears with me inside the rose. It looks like the one I lit before starting this imagery. I sit up, and the rose blossom opens completely. What I thought was the sun shining through the petals I see now are thousands of candles, seas of candles in every direction, shimmering like stars. It's stunningly beautiful. And then I hear a voice—or it's a message that gets relayed in some way, I'm not sure how. "Every time you lit a candle for meditation, for a dinner party, on a birthday cake, at Christmas, I have lit a hundred here for you." Just then, like a loud, roaring machine that gets unplugged, my heartache suddenly stops. The heaviness is gone. The silence is . . . palpable. I feel a deep stillness. It's like my heart is an open window to this vast space of light. I can't tell now whether the candles are inside my*

chest or outside of me. I want to live here forever. It's new and familiar at
the same time. The Voice that speaks to me feels like God, even though that
is not a word I use. It feels personal and everywhere. And so, so loving—it's
like a full-body understanding that I am not alone. The universe is me. God
is me. Or that It / Being is not separate from me. I can't find the right words,
but it's as close as I can get.

6. THANKING YOUR HEART (TWO MINUTES)

Thank your heart for the guidance it offered you and allow the image, sound, or impression to fade for now. Know that just as water can be moved from one room to another in a bowl, so too can you carry your heart's wisdom into your daily life in the vessel of your awareness.

Audrey's Thanks: *Namaste*

Take a moment in your sanctuary to notice your feelings that linger. Take a moment to let your body, mind, and emotions memorize whatever has been most valuable so that it will be very familiar and accessible to you.

Slowly open your eyes.

You will experience the greatest benefit from this process when your heart's wise advice guides your daily life experience. In the next few minutes you can integrate the wisdom you have discovered into your life by finding practical steps that transform your insight into action and presence.

DEEPENING YOUR UNDERSTANDING

Take your paper and turn it over with the blank side facing up. Write about or sketch your images and guidance. You may find that additional insights surface at this time. Your writing may simply be words or short phrases, or it may be a continual flow of thoughts and feelings. Don't be concerned about the writing structure. Allow yourself whatever form of expression comes most naturally in the moment.

Audrey's Insights: *I don't want to write, but I open my eyes and take time looking at the candle that I lit. There are tears flowing again, but they come from a different world. They are joyful. It's so strange, I want to laugh. It's like my inner eyes and outer eyes are open at the same time. I can see the candle in my room, but I can still see the ocean of candles, too. It's as though everything I see is lit from the inside by candlelight. And I can feel . . . um, God. I want to get comfortable with that name. I'm going to be with that Name now.*

BRINGING YOUR HEART'S WISDOM INTO DAILY LIFE

Is there a specific action you can take to integrate the guidance you just received into your life? Would it involve a conversation with someone or starting a daily practice? Is it about changing or letting go of a pattern? If so, decide specifically where, when, and how you will begin. What is the first step? Write it on your worksheet with the details of the timeline to which you will commit.

Or perhaps the wise advice from your heart is about a quality, such as patience or courage, that you want to cultivate more fully in your life. What are specific ways that you can stay connected to that quality throughout the day? Can you create touchstones to reconnect yourself to your heart's wisdom, such as putting a symbol on your desk or night-stand or taping a phrase from your writing to your bathroom mirror or dashboard?

Enjoy the wisdom your heart has given you!

Healing and Transformation through Self-Guided Imagery

Audrey's Plan: *The next morning I light a candle and sit down to go inward. As I settle in, I notice an enthusiastic little me that pops up in my head. She has a plan! "Let's light several candles in every room a couple of times a day." I can only love my industrious spiritual materialist who, so innocently, is eager to bump up our bank account with God. But for now, I take her by the hand, and we sit down together and close our eyes.*

EYES OPEN IMAGERY:
Cultivating an Awareness of Oneness

In the depth of her imagery journey, Audrey could no longer distinguish whether the candlelight was in her heart or her heart was in the candlelight. Like a Möbius strip that loses the clear boundary of inner and outer, her sense of self was turned inside out.

Did you know that *every* carbon atom in our bodies was once blasted from a star? With science confirming that we are indeed stardust, perhaps Audrey was close to the truth when it became unclear to her where we stop and start.

■ Notice your breath. At what point does it change from being the air around you to your breath—when it enters your body at the tip of your nose, halfway into your nasal passages, when it fills your lungs?

And when does the air around you stop being the sky—when you are in a room? What if the doors and windows are open? When does the sky stop being the space that stretches throughout the universe?

Breathe now without the names and divisions. Just experience this living image of breath that animates you.

■ Say your first name. Now find this person. Is she a mini-me in your brain with her hands on the levers of the control booth, peering out through your eyes? Is she your body? Was she there when you were ten, five, in the womb, in an egg or a sperm? Take a moment to find your self now.

But let's simplify. There are people; there is the world around us. Who would disagree with a description of everyday life as a world filled with sunshine, water, air, roads, trees, mountains, sounds, temperatures, and so forth? It's straightforward. Or is it? . . .

Take a flight of imagination and see the world as a bat would. Most bats see the world with their ears, that is, they use sound instead of light to perceive their environment. Step into bat reality for a moment: how would you describe this place now?

Or borrow the nose and ears of a dog, with the heightened sounds and scents that define the canine world, or experience the world according to a whale or an arctic worm. Do these creatures live in a completely different world because they have defective sensory organs and less complex brains? Or is "reality" simply defined by our particular sensory perceptions?

■ Lie down with your body being completely supported and comfortable. Cover your eyes with an eye pillow and use earplugs to eliminate sounds. What exists beyond the range of the frequencies that our eyes and ears can directly perceive? Be open to the living image of the invisible.

CHAPTER THREE

A SOURCE OF WISDOM THROUGH THE AGES

The greatest revolution of our generation
is the discovery that human beings, by changing
the inner attitudes of their minds, can change
the outer aspects of their lives.

WILLIAM JAMES

IT'S A CLEAR SUMMER NIGHT, and we gaze into the dark sky, blossoming with stars. In a thousand languages we utter: Who are we? Why are we here? Can we shape the world around us? Scientists, priests, poets, and those of us captivated by the beauty and terror of this world have pondered these questions. Guided imagery has emerged time and again as an essential tool for understanding and influencing life through-out the history of humanity. Because it is a natural, accessible way of knowing, it is befitting that guided imagery has arisen within medicine, science, psychology, spiritual practice, and optimal athletic performance. The pervasiveness and widespread influence of guided imagery speaks not only to the powerful nature of imagery but also to its inherent role within human experience. Let's take a brief historical tour with early explorers of the imagination and start by traveling to Germany in the year 1895.

At the speed of light, we jump centuries and find ourselves peering through an open window of a simple wooden house. There sits a teen-ager, sixteen years old, lost in a daydream. His head rests on the palm of his hand, eyes closed, his wild hair uncombed. Let's zoom in even closer and join him in his visualization. This boy is imagining what it would be like to ride on a beam of light. Mathematician Jacques Hadamard, in his book *The Psychology of Invention in the Mathematical Field,* includes a let-ter he received from Albert Einstein, who describes how his prolonged daydream led to his famous formulation of the theory of special relativity in 1905. One of the greatest scientific minds of our times, Einstein was interviewed in 1929 by George Sylvester Viereck of the *Saturday Evening Post.* He was quoted as saying, "Imagination is more important than knowledge. For knowledge is limited to all we now know and under-stand, where imagination embraces the entire world, and all there ever will be to know and understand."

Although we tend to think of science as logical and based on the observable, quantum physics in particular requires utilizing the imagi-native capacities of the mind because it deals with the invisible. It goes beyond the scope of direct sensory experience. In *The Ascent of Man,* mathematician Jacob Bronowski states, "When we step through the gate-way of the atom, we are in a world which our senses cannot experience. There is a new architecture there, a way that things are put together which we cannot know; we only try to picture it by analogy, a new act of imagination." Niels Bohr, winner of the Nobel Prize in quantum mechan-ics, is attributed in Steven Giles's book, *Theorizing Modernism: Essays in Critical Theory,* as saying, "When it comes to atoms, language can be used only as in poetry. The poet, too, is not nearly as concerned with describ-ing facts as with creating images."

If we remain in the year 1895 and travel south to the University of Basel in Switzerland, we find a serious, introverted young man; just twenty years of age, studying archaeology before going into psychiatric medicine. Another brilliant mind and influential thinker, Carl Gustav

Jung significantly shaped the practice of psychology as we know it today, with a strong conviction of the importance of the imagination for living a full and meaningful life. Jung devoted much of his life to exploring images that arise from the unconscious. He believed that accessing these images and integrating their meaning is necessary in order to experience life fully. In the *C. G. Jung Letter, Vol. 1: 1906–1950*, Jung states, "Your vision will become clear only when you look into your heart. Who looks outside, dreams. Who looks within, awakens."

Jung developed an approach called *active imagination* to help people tap into these internal realms. Jung's writings are beautifully compiled by editor Joan Chodorow in *Jung on Active Imagination*. He didn't consider these layers of consciousness to be imaginary in the sense of being unreal. Rather, he recognized images as the natural language of the psyche. In *Memories, Dreams, Reflections*, he writes, "There are things in the psyche which I do not produce, but which produce themselves and have their own life. . . . Their autonomy is a most uncomfortable thing to reconcile oneself to, and yet the very fact that the unconscious presents itself in that way gives us the best means of handling it."

Imagery also found its way into other psychotherapeutic approaches, such as cognitive-behavioral therapy. Aaron Beck, a psychiatrist considered to be the father of cognitive therapy, applies imagery techniques to diminish anxiety in patients. Because Beck recognized that worrying is a form of imagery, he taught patients how to interrupt negative images playing in the mind and replace them with positive ones.

This approach was further developed in the 1960s by psychiatrist Joseph Wolpe, who blended relaxation and imagery to treat phobias. This technique directs the person to gradually imagine increasingly stressful circumstances while also increasing the ability to relax. Eventually the patient is conditioned to replace anxious feelings with relaxing ones, even in the most anxiety-provoking situations.

A specialized application of imagery has recently emerged in the field of optimal athletic performance. The accomplished golfer Jack Nicklaus describes his use of imagery in his autobiography, *Golf My Way*. "I never hit a shot, even in practice, without having a very sharp, in-focus picture of it in my head. It's like a color movie. I see the ball where I want it to finish, its path, trajectory, even its behavior on landing. Then I see me making the swing that will make the image a reality. Only then do I pick a club and step up to the ball."

One of the most impressive research studies in this area is cited in *The Cambridge Handbook of Expertise and Expert Performance*. Included is a study by neurologist Dr. Alvaro Pascual-Leone at the Universidad de Valencia in Spain, which demonstrated that visualizations were more powerful than physical practice for improving students' basketball free-throw scores. The study used four groups of randomly selected college students who were first measured for their basic skill level. Each group received different instructions.

Group one: The control group was to do nothing different from their routines that related to basketball during the duration of the study.

Group two: This group was instructed to practice shooting free throws for a half-hour each day.

Group three: Each member of this group was instructed not to touch a basketball during this time, but to commit a half-hour each day to imagining making free throws.

Group four: This group practiced free throws for fifteen minutes each day and visualized free throws for fifteen minutes each day.

At the end of the study, each group was tested for improvement. Group four showed the most improvement, blending imagery with practice. Group three made the second biggest improvement, with those who practiced only in the imagination outperforming those who actually practiced shooting free throws each day.

This study brings us again to the clear understanding that images in the mind bring about changes in the body. So it should come as no surprise that imagery has a role to play in medicine. Guided imagery programs are part of hospital practices across the country, including those at California Pacific Medical Center in San Francisco, the Mayo Clinic in New York, the Washington Hospital Centers, and Hartford Hospital in Connecticut, to name just a few.

The success of guided imagery is widely documented in the medical field. Growing research shows that guided imagery can produce healing effects on the cardiovascular and immune functions, reduce pain, alter brainwave patterns, and provide many other benefits. Imagery impacts the autonomic nervous system, usually considered to be outside the realm of conscious influence. Imagery is known to decrease headaches by up to 62 percent, enhance sleep by as much as 75 percent, and decrease pulmonary symptoms (such as asthma, allergies, emphysema), and there are more than seventy-five studies related to the benefits of guided imagery during cancer treatment.

Two hallmark studies, both conducted at the Cleveland Clinic, document the powerful effect of imagery in combination with contemporary medicine procedures. The first study, under the direction of Dr. Victor Fazio and Dr. James Church in the Colorectal Surgery Department, prepares patients for major surgery using imagery. Published in the medical journal *Diseases of the Colon and Rectum*, the research shows a 65 percent decrease in pain and anxiety, 33 percent fewer side effects, and 75 percent overall patient satisfaction as compared to patients who did not use the imagery support. Although the patient populations are entirely different, a similar imagery preparation was used with cardiothoracic surgery, under the direction of Dr. Delos Cosgrove. The results of the study, published in *The Journal of Cardiovascular Management*, showed that the patients had virtually identical benefits using imagery for their surgery preparation and recovery.

But imagery is not new to the healing arts. Although we now have the research to verify the validity of guided imagery, the power of imagery has been known instinctually for centuries. In Franz Hartmann's book *Paracelsus: Life and Prophecies*, the sixteenth-century physician Paracelsus stated, "The power of the imagination is a great factor in medicine. It may produce diseases in man, and it may cure them." Originally copyrighted in 1850, Dr. James Esdaile's book, *Hypnosis in Medicine and Surgery*, describes how he performed almost four hundred surgeries, including those on eyes, ears, and throats, as well as amputations and tumor removals using "mental anesthesia" for pain control. It is recorded that his patients reported a zero pain level with his "hypnoanesthesia."

Although research has validated the effectiveness of guided imagery, let's fly again through space and time to Greece in the second century and discover how guided imagery is actually ancient wisdom.

It's midafternoon, and the sun makes brilliant patches of slowly traveling white light across the tiles of an open-air courtyard. The scent of the sea makes the air fresh and comfortably moist. Three men in beige and tan tunics are gesturing, very engaged in a lively conversation as they pour over the writing of the *Corpus Hermeticus*, one of the earliest texts devoted to exploring the nature of life.

These essential questions about life often examine the relationship between our inner world and outer reality. Although the *Corpus Hermeticus* was likely written in the second century, some scholars speculate that the Hermetic philosophy may trace back to the second millennium BC in pharaonic Egypt. Hermetic philosophy, as described by anonymous authors in *The Kybalion: A Study of the Hermetic Philosophy of Ancient Egypt and Greece*, describes a source of life referred to as "the All," or the "Supreme Good," which mentally projects the universe in the same way that people create mental images. Hermes took this further in describing life as an interconnected system in which a specific image held in the mind will produce changes in the physical universe. This ancient philosophy actually describes a foundational concept practiced in contemporary mind-body medicine!

An essential link between a mental cause and a physical effect has been proven with recent research in psychoneuroimmunology. For example, if you are sitting in a quiet, safe environment, but your mind is filled with vivid images of an argument that occurred yesterday, scores of measurable impacts occur in your body's physiology based solely on the impact of the images. A rise in blood pressure, an increase in muscular tension, and elevated cortisol levels in the blood can be measured. The mental images have greater impact on the body than the reality of a quiet, external environment. The journal *Cerebral Cortex*, published by Oxford University Press, published the article "Neural Substrates of Real and Imagined Sensorimotor Coordination." This research revealed that the same neural pathways in the brain were firing whether an event was actually physically performed or only imagined. With the brain registering imagined events and events in the physical environment in exactly the same way, it's no wonder that our thoughts have such an impact on our physiological and emotional states.

The basic premise that internal images create subtle and physical change is the same principle understood by religious traditions that use guided imagery. In a spiritual context, the images are typically very precise, directing practitioners to create specific religious experiences. For example, if we could drop in on colorful sixth-century India, we would see how tantric yoga, which influenced both Hinduism and Buddhism, teaches practitioners to imagine a sacred image. Within Tantrism, the visualized symbols are often particular deities. It is believed that concentration on a sacred image creates a pipeline for the divine attributes to be experienced directly by the practitioner, activating latent spiritual energies within and ultimately leading to an experience of union with the divine.

A similar use of guided imagery is described in early Christian contemplative prayer. John Cassian, recognized as a saint in both the Roman Catholic and the Eastern Orthodox Churches, built an Egyptian-style monastery near Marseille, where he taught a three-step path to mysticism that culminates in the use of divine imagery. In his fourth-century book *Collationes*, he describes the "training of the inner man and the perfection of the heart." The final stage, *Unitio*, involves the practitioner filling his or her purified heart with an image of Christ, which leads to a union between the Spirit of God and the soul of the practitioner.

This early Christian practice is further articulated in the fourteenth-century book *The Cloud of Unknowing*. The anonymous author articulates a theological perspective that requires clearing the mind of rational thought in order to be able to truly experience the presence of the sacred within. Here the author is describing the liminal space (defined in Chapter 2) where images arise. From this perspective, any time we believe that we "know" what God is, that seeming knowledge crystallizes into a thought form that actually blocks us from directly experiencing the divine.

The nature of God, regardless of what name is used to describe it, appears in a variety of spiritual traditions as a living reality that exists beyond thoughts. In the Jewish religion, God as creator of the universe exists outside of space and time. Stephen Mitchell's translation of the primary text of the Taoist tradition, *Tao Te Ching*, states that the truth "which can be told is not the eternal Tao. The name that can be named is not the eternal Name." The Taittiriya hymn of Hinduism, as translated by Chand Devi in *Yajurveda*, speaks of Brahman, the Supreme Spirit, as "one where the mind does not reach."

But let's travel back even further in time, twenty thousand years, and head again to the south of France and peer into what are now called the Les Trois Frères caves.

In the flickering firelight, the rough edges of the cave look dark and mottled through the hazy air. A stocky, muscular man crouches forward, his strong hand slowly etching and staining graceful line drawings of bison, deer, and other wild creatures into a smooth section of rock. The movement and vitality these drawing express is stunning. The central drawing is a figure about two and a half feet tall. Strange and mysterious, the head of this figure sprouts deer antlers and has owl-like eyes above a dark beard. With paws for hands and the tail of a fox, here stands the part human, part animal shaman of Trois Frères.

Shamanism, practiced in North and South America, Asia, Africa, Australia, and Europe, is the oldest and most widespread tradition that uses images for healing. As with so many of the world traditions we have looked at, shamanistic worldview holds that there's a bridge between the spirit realm and the day-to-day world, created by shamanic practices that shift awareness out of the ordinary thinking mind. Within shamanism, this change in consciousness is referred to as a trance or journey, and the practice often incorporates dancing, drumming, and meditating. By entering realms of the imagination through trance, spirit guides, power animals, and healing symbols are invoked.

But let us now turn our focus from the past to the present and discover the amazing world of imagery that lies within each of us. In their book, *Ideation: The Birth and Death of Ideas*, Douglas Graham and Thomas Bachman quote Michelangelo as having said, "I saw the angel in the marble and carved until I set him free." As we learn the methods for seeing into our own hearts, we can set free the images and angels awaiting us there.

LEONARD: CANCER

*You ask why I make my home in the
mountain forest, and I smile, and am silent,
and even my soul remains quiet: it lives in
the other world which no one owns.*

LI PO

LEONARD IS A FORMIDABLE PRESENCE with a firm hand-
shake and a clear, direct gaze. An African American lawyer in his late fif-
ties, he was recently diagnosed with a rare cancer that showed up under
his sternum. Because this is an unusual type of cancer, there are no established treatment protocols. Although cancer treatment always has some
element of trial and error, this uncharted territory requires a particularly creative and intelligent intervention on the part of an oncologist.
Leonard finds comfort in requiring a unique medical approach rather
than being a routine subject for a clinical pathway and has found a medical team he trusts that is up to taking on this challenge.

He has everything to live for. He finds meaning in his work, but the
deepest motivation to beat this disease is fueled by his truly supportive
family. His lovely wife is his best friend and advocate, and they have two
smart teenagers. It's an honest household—no secrets. And although no
one can walk his path for him, they are in this together all the way.

Leonard is determined to rally all possible resources to overcome
his cancer, in spite of the fact that his doctors offer a grim prognosis. He

has been reading about imagery and listening to some imagery CDs but wants to be sure he is enlisting the most proven, effective ways to bring his inner resources to bear as supplemental treatment.

Leonard's well-honed, analytical mind is one of his greatest assets. It has lifted him into high-profile success. He has also meditated off and on for much of his adult life. He's been one, like many of us, who so often recommits to meditating on a regular schedule but has found that it gets squeezed out of the day much more often than intended.

Although in no way traditionally religious, Leonard has sensed what he describes as "another force," something that directs life beyond what is easily explainable. He has often felt this force during meditation and feels strongly that it has something to offer his healing.

And yet, even with valuable personal experience with meditation and research backing the efficacy of guided imagery, Leonard's logical side exerts criticism at the part of him shaping his healing plan to include guided imagery. "It's just gallows thinking, Leonard. You are grasping at straws. Don't make a fool of yourself." Even with his "guardian of the rational" muscling its way in, Leonard still chooses to start doing guided imagery on a daily basis, intensifying the practice to almost three hours a day.

The rational and intuitive aspects of his mind often argue and flip-flop, first finding the imagery journeys tremendously valuable and then questioning whether it is a waste of time. Finding a way to integrate these two valuable ways of knowing, the rational and the intuitive, especially as it relates to his healing journey, becomes a significant theme for Leonard.

At times, Leonard has a strong sense that incorporating a deeper connection with this force is even bigger than the question of whether it will support a cure for his cancer. He started seeing in retrospect how his long-term interest in imagery and meditation has been like a coffee-table travel book that he loves but rarely opens. But now it's walk-your-talk time, the stakes are high, and he wants to not only open the book but also traverse those landscapes.

Leonard frequently uses his imagery sessions to consult with his inner healer, Li Po. Here is one of Leonard's imagery journeys that marks a pivotal insight in his healing practice.

Journey to the Wisdom of the Heart
SELF-FACILITATION WORKSHEET

1. WHAT DO YOU NEED GUIDANCE ABOUT? (ONE MINUTE)

Write one word or phrase to stand for the topic on which you wish to receive inner guidance from your heart. Make it as short as possible. For example, if your concern is "My ex-husband is late again with a child-support payment. He breaks his agreements time and again. What shall I do?" you would write "my ex" or "finances," depending on which is closest to your real concern.

Write the word or phrase on the piece of paper. Turn the paper over and set it aside, trusting that in just a few minutes, a greater wisdom than you now possess will fully address your concern.

Leonard's Topic: *Healing*

2. JOURNEY TO YOUR HEART BY TRAVELING INWARD (THREE TO FOUR MINUTES)

The journey to your heart begins as soon as you close your eyes. Bring your attention to your breathing. Each time you breathe in, silently say the word *clarity*. Every time you exhale, silently say the word *peace* and feel your body relaxing. Any time you find your thoughts wandering, bring your focus back to your breath and relaxation. Continue for about three minutes, until you are as relaxed as possible.

Leonard's Journey: *I drop my attention into my abdomen. I follow the movement of breath there. Then I just step back, moving into an open space.*

3. DISCOVERING YOUR INNER SANCTUARY (THREE MINUTES)

Now that you're relaxed, imagine a place where you can feel even more peaceful. It may be a beach, a meadow, or a quiet room in your home. It could even be an imaginary place. Whatever appears, let it be a setting where you can be completely yourself, free from pressures or expectations. You may be surprised where you find yourself, but let your heart show you where it wants to meet you. Even if you have done this process before, you may find yourself in a new environment that is just right for today. Whether you are indoors or outdoors, settle into the most comfortable spot and enjoy the colors, sounds, scents, and feel of this safe and special place.

Leonard's Inner Sanctuary: *I'm in Sedona, Arizona. I've been here in imagery and in life several times. The land has naturally carved rock formations striped in reds and tans. I am in a particular spot where I feel an energy vortex. It's an open space surrounded by a semicircle of rock formations. The land here has a hum. I sit directly in the center and close my eyes.*

4. BRINGING YOUR TOPIC TO HEART (ONE MINUTE)

Now imagine your paper being delivered to you in this wonderful place. In your mind's eye, view your concern again. Feel your distress embraced by the qualities of your inner sanctuary. Imagine holding your paper and concern lightly in your upturned palms and know that you are about to receive clear guidance from your heart.

Leonard's Topic: *Healing*

5. RECEIVING YOUR HEART'S MESSAGE
(THREE TO FIVE MINUTES)

In your sanctuary, ask your heart for a wise and loving response to your issue. Let your heart's reply appear as an image a few feet in front of you. Whatever symbol appears, receive it as an honored guest. Whether it is a color, a figure, a phrase, or an impression, notice its texture, shape, sound, and so on. Feel the qualities that this image embodies. What does it want you to know about your concern? How do you feel in the presence of your heart's wise advice?

Leonard's Heart's Message: *I invite my inner healer, Li Po, to join me as he has done so many times. He is here now and is in traditional Chinese garb. We greet each other, and I thank him for coming. I want his advice on whether I'm on track with my healing. He tells me I have done very well, but it is time for a deeper practice. He explains to me that the way I'm approaching my healing is a reproduction of the way I do almost everything in my life. It's time for my foundational way of doing things to change, and it needs to start with this healing practice. He says that my pattern is to fight to overcome adversity and that healing is not a war. He asks me if I understand. I'm a little uncertain about his perspective, since the imagery I've been reading about encourages waging a successful battle against disease. This guided imagery approach is backed by solid research, which I find reassuring. I tell Li Po that I have a sense of what he's saying but I'm also uncomfortable and would like to know more. He explains to me that I need to participate fully but that it is not about exerting my will. He advises me to feel my wholeness and follow that feeling to its Source. He tells me I will find a power much greater than my will. It is the same power that draws me to Sedona, the same impulse that keeps drawing me into this practice, and it is what I truly seek for healing. Li Po asks me if I would like to experience this now. I agree, and we meditate together. This is the first time that the focus is not specifically on imagining my cancer and immune system, but rather on a feeling of vital well-being that lives around, or through, everything else. I bring my attention fully into my sense of well-being, wholeness, and I feel light, vast, clear, and buoyant. We complete the meditation and I ask him, "Who are you? Are you a representation of the force?" He replies simply that my name for him is not quite accurate, but he knows that it makes sense for me to think of him that way. That feels good enough for me. I don't want to know more right now. I feel very light and full.*

6. THANKING YOUR HEART (TWO MINUTES)

Thank your heart for the guidance it offered you and allow the image, sound, or impression to fade for now. Know that just as water can be moved from one room to another in a bowl, so too can you carry your heart's wisdom into your daily life in the vessel of your awareness.

Leonard's Thanks: *Thank you, Li Po.*

Take a moment in your sanctuary to notice your feelings that linger. Take a moment to let your body, mind, and emotions memorize whatever hs been most valuable so that it will be very familiar and accessible to you.

Slowly open your eyes.

You will experience the greatest benefit from this process when your heart's wise advice guides your daily life experience. In the next few minutes you can integrate the wisdom you discovered into your life by finding practical steps that transform your insight into action and presence.

DEEPENING YOUR UNDERSTANDING

Take your paper and turn it over with the blank side facing up. Write about or sketch your images and guidance. You may find that additional insights surface at this time. Your writing may simply be words or short phrases, or it may be a continual flow of thoughts and feelings. Don't be concerned about the writing structure. Allow yourself whatever form of expression comes most naturally in the moment.

Leonard's Insights: *I have always benefited by following Li Po's advice before, and I am going to take his guidance to heart. I can see how my approach has been a battlefield between me and my disease, and he is asking me to step into a much larger arena with a new orientation entirely. It felt absolutely confirming when I was experiencing it. I need time to integrate this and will reenter the experience in tomorrow's guided imagery.*

BRINGING YOUR HEART'S WISDOM INTO DAILY LIFE

Is there a specific action you can take to integrate the guidance you just received into your life? Would it involve a conversation with someone or starting a daily practice? Is it about changing or letting go of a pattern? If so, decide specifically where, when, and how you will begin. What is the first step? Write it on your worksheet with the details of the timeline to which you will commit.

Or perhaps the wise advice from your heart is about a quality, such as patience or courage, that you want to cultivate more fully in your life. What are specific ways that you can stay connected to that quality throughout the day? Can you create touchstones to reconnect yourself to your heart's wisdom, such as putting a symbol on your desk or nightstand or taping a phrase from your writing to your bathroom mirror or dashboard?

Enjoy the wisdom your heart has given you!

Leonard's Plan: *My main task is to make sure that I carve out time to enter the meditative imagery experience on a daily basis. My directive is to spend time experiencing my wholeness. I am committed to accomplishing this.*

Cultivating an Awareness of Openness

You have probably heard the old saying, "You can't really understand another person's experience until you've walked a mile in their shoes." This is a practice in stepping into those other shoes. It is not about figuring out what is the correct point of view or strategizing how to finally convince the other that you are right. It is about exploring, expanding understanding, and loosening emotional gridlock.

■ Focus on a situation in your life where there is a conflict—you and your health, you and a disagreement with your partner, you and an unresolved situation with your boss. Notice the adversarial nature of the situation, feeling the ways you defend your point of view, bolster your feelings, and fearfully wonder how you can win.

Enter, as fully as you can, the other person's experience or situation. Look at yourself through her eyes. Write out how you see yourself through her eyes and what the "other" wants to say to you. Take your time to really flip 180 degrees and step "into" the adversary. Every situation is unique. If the adversary is something like cancer, it might start like this:

Sample: *I am in darkness. Pay attention to me. Look at me. I know I seem strong to you, but I am confused. I am confused cells, and I have lost my way.*

Once you have written out the adversary's point of view, come back to yourself and be with what you have heard and seen. Is there anything surprising to you? Do you see anything new about yourself or the "other"? Has the feeling tone shifted in any way? What does the "other" really want and need? Now write out your response to the "other" but start with restating what you understand it wants you to know. Really notice what feels true to you now, and respond from there. Stay aligned with your own integrity.

- Alice Calaprice's *The New Quotable Einstein* attributes Einstein with saying, "The significant problems we face cannot be solved at the same level of thinking we were at when we created them." How can you shift levels? One way is to shift the framework entirely.

Staying with the original conflict that you have been exploring, allow everything about it to remain the same, but eliminate the framework that it is a "problem." Instead, it could be the conditions you find yourself in or simply the current situation. This is not a play on words or just sugarcoating a dilemma. Really take some time to imagine how your life situation would be right now without the thought that it is a problem.

This is not about being passive. In fact, you may find that there is even greater clarity and energy for saying something or taking action. Or it may become clear that nothing is needed right now.

- Look at the person or situation as a living image. What is it expressing to you right now?

CHAPTER FOUR

JOURNEY TO THE WISDOM OF YOUR HEART:

A SELF-FACILITATION GUIDE

We must close our eyes and invoke a new manner of seeing . . .
A wakefulness that is the birthright of us all.

PLOTINUS

THIS IS A SIMPLE, six-step guided imagery process that can bring you to your heart's wise guidance. You can use the worksheet by yourself any time you want clarity and relief from concerns. All you need is a piece of paper and a pen or pencil.

Although this worksheet provides everything you need to take you directly to your wisdom within, chapters 5, 6, 7, 8, and 9 offer additional tools that allow you to fine-tune your imagery journey. The chapter titles match the steps of the worksheet so that it is easy to find what you are looking for. For example, you may find the breathing exercise in step 2 of the worksheet completely relaxing. But if you are someone who relaxes more easily with a different approach, you can replace it with one of the many exercises for traveling inward presented in Chapter 6. Or perhaps the walking meditation or music practice would be a better fit for you.

The chapters listed on page 47 also offer solutions to concerns that occasionally arise. Let's say you are fully relaxed and ready to enter your inner sanctuary. You follow the steps but find there is no image. Or there are three beautiful places that come to mind. Or it's a scary place rather than a peaceful one. Now what do you do? Chapter 7, Discovering Your Inner Sanctuary, gives you the solutions for overcoming these temporary obstacles and continuing your imagery journey.

So let's begin. It is important to read *all* the steps of this worksheet before you start. You also have the option of prerecording the instructions or having a friend read them to you aloud. Be sure to follow the suggestions for pacing noted by each step. You can also download free MP3s of the worksheet at www.LeslieDavenport.com.

Whichever version you choose, set aside twenty minutes in a quiet, comfortable setting where you will not be interrupted. Find a relaxed position, whether lying down, sitting in a chair, or supported by cushions.

Journey to the Wisdom of the Heart
SELF-FACILITATION WORKSHEET

1. WHAT DO YOU NEED GUIDANCE ABOUT? (ONE MINUTE)

Write one word or phrase to stand for the topic on which you wish to receive inner guidance from your heart. Make it as short as possible. For example, if your concern is "My ex-husband is late again with a child-support payment. He breaks his agreements time and again. What shall I do?" you would write "my ex" or "finances," depending on which is closest to your real concern.

Write the word or phrase on the piece of paper. Turn the paper over and set it aside, trusting that in just a few minutes, a greater wisdom than you now possess will fully address your concern.

Your Topic: ....

2. JOURNEY TO YOUR HEART BY TRAVELING INWARD (THREE TO FOUR MINUTES)

The journey to your heart begins as soon as you close your eyes. Bring your attention to your breathing. Each time you breathe in, silently say the word *clarity*. Every time you exhale, silently say the word *peace* and feel your body relaxing. Any time you find your thoughts wandering, bring your focus back to your breath and relaxation. Continue for about three minutes, until you are as relaxed as possible.

Your Journey: ....
....
....

3. DISCOVERING YOUR INNER SANCTUARY (THREE MINUTES)

Now that that you're relaxed, imagine a place where you can feel even more peaceful. It may be a beach, a meadow, or a quiet room in your home. It could even be an imaginary place. Whatever appears, let it be a setting where you can be completely yourself, free from pressures or expectations. You may be surprised where you find yourself, but let your heart show you where it wants to meet you. Even if you have done this process before, you may find yourself in a new environment that is just right for today. Whether you are indoors or outdoors, settle into the most comfortable spot, and enjoy the colors, sounds, scents, and feel of this safe and special place.

Your Inner Sanctuary: ....
....
....

4. BRINGING YOUR TOPIC TO HEART (ONE MINUTE)

Now imagine your paper being delivered to you in this wonderful place. In your mind's eye, view your concern again. Feel your distress embraced by the qualities of your inner sanctuary. Imagine holding your paper and concern lightly in your upturned palms and know that you are about to receive clear guidance from your heart.

Revisiting Your Topic: ....
....
....

Healing and Transformation through Self-Guided Imagery

5. RECEIVING YOUR HEART'S MESSAGE (THREE TO FIVE MINUTES)

In your sanctuary, ask your heart for a wise and loving response to your issue. Let your heart's reply appear as an image a few feet in front of you. Whatever symbol appears, receive it as an honored guest. Whether it is a color, a figure, a phrase, or an impression, notice its texture, shape, sound, and so on. Feel the qualities that this image embodies. What does it want you to know about your concern? How do you feel in the presence of your heart's wise advice?

Your Heart's Message: ....
....
....
....
....
....
....
....
....
....
....

6. THANKING YOUR HEART (TWO MINUTES)

Thank your heart for the guidance it offered you and allow the image, sound, or impression to fade for now. Know that just as water can be moved from one room to another in a bowl, so too can you carry your heart's wisdom into your daily life in the vessel of your awareness.

Your Thanks: ....
....
....

Take a moment in your sanctuary to notice your feelings that linger. Take a moment to let your body, mind, and emotions memorize whatever has been most valuable so that it will be very familiar and accessible to you.

Slowly open your eyes.

You will experience the greatest benefit from this process when your heart's wise advice guides your daily life experience. In the next few minutes you can integrate the wisdom you discovered into your life by finding practical steps that transform your insight into action and presence.

DEEPENING YOUR UNDERSTANDING

Turn your paper over with the blank side facing up. Write about or sketch your images and guidance. You may find that additional insights surface at this time. Your writing may simply be words or short phrases, or it may be a continual flow of thoughts and feelings. Don't be concerned about the writing structure. Allow yourself whatever form of expression comes most naturally in the moment.

Your Insights: ....
....
....

BRINGING YOUR HEART'S WISDOM INTO DAILY LIFE

Is there a specific action you can take to integrate the guidance you just received into your life? Would it involve a conversation with someone or starting a daily practice? Is it about changing or letting go of a pattern? If so, decide specifically where, when, and how you will begin. What is the first step? Write it on your worksheet with the details of the timeline to which you will commit.

Or perhaps the wise advice from your heart is about a quality, such as patience or courage, that you want to cultivate more fully in your life. What are specific ways that you can stay connected to that quality throughout the day? Can you create touchstones to reconnect yourself to your heart's wisdom, such as putting a symbol on your desk or nightstand or taping a phrase from your writing to your bathroom mirror or dashboard?

Enjoy the wisdom your heart has given you!

Your Plan: ....
....
....

SHARON: IMMOBILITY— FEAR OF CHANGE

And the day came when the risk it took to
remain tight inside the bud was more painful
than the risk it took to bloom.

ANAÏS NIN

EVERYONE SEEMS TO exhale a little when they are near Sharon. She has a soft glow that falls on everything around her. Maybe it's the way she seems so completely incapable of doing harm to anyone or anything. She's quiet, a listener. And she takes you in with her big blue eyes. In her early forties, she has delicate bones and fair features. Her baby-fine straight hair, so blonde it is almost white, is evidence of her family's Norwegian heritage. Her manner communicates reassurance.

Almost no one can detect the distress hidden behind her truly gracious demeanor. The only hint is the occasional doelike stance, when she's frozen just for a moment, which stems from vigilant attentiveness to her social environment. She's always ready to smooth things out and help others feel comfortable.

This gentle way of being has become both a gift and a prison to Sharon. Although so many enjoy her calm presence, it is virtually her only mode of expression out of the full scope of human emotions. Like trying to paint a portrait with only one color, Sharon was feeling up against the limitations of her way of being in the world. She has been very unhappy with her relationship and her work situation for quite some time, but she has kept these feelings tucked away in her own private world. Qualities and behaviors such as assertive strength and tolerating conflict have been banished from her life, and she needs additional inner resources now in order to initiate change.

She had begun to recognize the building pressure of her unhappiness and she chose to do a self-facilitated guided imagery session on her immobility.

Journey to the Wisdom of the Heart
SELF-FACILITATION WORKSHEET

This is a simple process you can use by yourself any time you want clarity and relief from concerns. All you need is a piece of paper and a pen or pencil.

It is important to read *all* the steps before you begin. You also have the option of prerecording the instructions or having a friend read them to you aloud. There are suggestions for timing noted by each step. You can also download a prerecorded version of this session from my website at no cost.

Whichever version you choose, set aside twenty minutes in a quiet, comfortable setting where you will not be interrupted. Find a relaxed position, whether lying down, sitting in a chair, or supported by cushions.

1. WHAT DO YOU NEED GUIDANCE ABOUT? (ONE MINUTE)

Write one word or phrase to stand for the topic on which you wish to receive inner guidance from your heart. Make it as short as possible. For example, if your concern is "My ex-husband is late again with a child-support payment. He breaks his agreements time and again.

What shall I do?" you would write "my ex" or "finances," depending on which is closest to your real concern.

Write the word or phrase on the piece of paper. Turn the paper over and set it aside, trusting that in just a few minutes, a greater wisdom than you now possess will fully address your concern.

Sharon's Topic: *Immobility*

2. JOURNEY TO YOUR HEART BY TRAVELING INWARD (THREE TO FOUR MINUTES)

The journey to your heart begins as soon as you close your eyes. Bring your attention to your breathing. Each time you breathe in, silently say the word *clarity*. Every time you exhale, silently say the word *peace* and feel your body relaxing. Anytime you find your thoughts wandering, bring your focus back to your breath and relaxation. Continue for about three minutes, until you are as relaxed as possible.

Sharon's Journey: *It took me a while to settle in, but I started with feeling the expansion of my belly as I breathed in, and feeling my belly settle as I breathed out. It began to feel like the ebb and flow of the ocean.*

3. DISCOVERING YOUR INNER SANCTUARY (THREE MINUTES)

Now that you're relaxed, imagine a place where you can feel even more peaceful. It may be a beach, a meadow, or a quiet room in your home. It could even be an imaginary place. Whatever appears, let it be a setting where you can be completely yourself, free from pressures or expectations. Where you find yourself may surprise you, but let your heart show you where it wants to meet you. Even if you have done this process before, you may find yourself in a new environment that is just right for today. Whether you find yourself indoors or outdoors, settle into the most comfortable spot and enjoy the colors, sounds, scents, and feel of this safe and special place.

Sharon's Inner Sanctuary: *I'm on a tropical, deserted beach at dawn. Even though it is early and the sun is just rising, the air is moist and comfortable, almost 70 degrees. I hear only the surf and an occasional bird song. The water is glassy out past gentle breakers. It's greenish and clear, and the sand is speckled whites, tans, and brown. I'm facing the sunrise, and although the sky is beginning to fill with shifting pinks, yellows, and orange, it feels simple and ordinary in a way. I can't explain it—spectacular but quiet. I feel very strong and calm, like the sea.*

4. BRINGING YOUR TOPIC TO HEART (ONE MINUTE)

Now imagine your paper being delivered to you in this wonderful place. In your mind's eye, view your concern again. Feel your distress embraced by the qualities of your inner sanctuary. Imagine holding your paper and concern lightly in your upturned palms and know that you are about to receive clear guidance from your heart.

Sharon's Topic: *Immobility*

5. RECEIVING YOUR HEART'S MESSAGE (THREE TO FIVE MINUTES)

In your sanctuary, ask your heart for a wise and loving response to your issue. Let your heart's reply appear as an image a few feet in front of you. Whatever symbol appears, receive it as an honored guest. Whether it is a color, a figure, a phrase, or an impression, notice its texture, shape, sound, and so on. Feel the qualities that this image embodies. What does it want you to know about your concern? How do you feel in the presence of your heart's wise advice?

Sharon's Heart's Message: *The image that appears is that of a baby parrot. It's sitting on a bare wooden branch. Its feathers are vibrant green, red, and blue in color. The parrot is quiet, glancing at me, then away, and then back again. It reminds me of a story I heard or read long ago about a man at an outdoor market in Mexico who had many parrots on perches, uncaged, with him. When a passerby asked why the birds did not fly away, he replied, "Because they do not know that they can." I can feel that little parrot wants me to know that I can fly, I can move.*

6. THANKING YOUR HEART (TWO MINUTES)

Thank your heart for the guidance it offered you and allow the image, sound, or impression to fade for now. Know that just as water can be moved from one room to another in a bowl, so too can you carry your heart's wisdom into your daily life in the vessel of your awareness.

Sharon's Thanks: *Thank you, my own sweet heart. I feel quite inspired and awestruck by the appearance of this symbol, my heart's response. I am filled with gratitude.*

Take a moment in your sanctuary to notice your feelings that linger. Take a moment to let your body, mind, and emotions memorize whatever has been most valuable so that it will be very familiar and accessible to you.

Slowly open your eyes.

You will experience the greatest benefit from this process when your heart's wise advice guides your daily life experience. In the next few minutes you can integrate the wisdom you have discovered into your life by finding practical steps that transform your insight into action and presence.

DEEPENING YOUR UNDERSTANDING

Take your paper and turn it over with the blank side facing up. Write about or sketch your images and guidance. You may find that additional insights surface at this time. Your writing may simply be words or short phrases, or it may be a continual flow of thoughts and feelings. Don't be concerned about the writing structure. Allow yourself whatever form of expression comes most naturally in the moment.

Sharon's Insights: *I feel the advice from my heart is to cultivate the courage to move and to do just as I would want the parrots to move and to do.*

BRINGING YOUR HEART'S WISDOM INTO DAILY LIFE

Is there a specific action you can take to integrate the guidance you just received into your life? Would it involve a conversation with someone or starting a daily practice? Is it about changing or letting go of a pattern? If so, decide specifically where, when, and how you will begin. What is the first step? Write it on your paper with the details of the timeline to which you will commit.

Or perhaps the wise advice from your heart is about a quality, such as patience or courage, that you want to cultivate more fully in your life. What are specific ways that you can stay connected to that quality throughout the day? Can you create touchstones to reconnect yourself to your heart's wisdom, such as putting a symbol on your desk or nightstand or taping a phrase from your writing to your bathroom mirror or dashboard?

Enjoy the wisdom your heart has given you!

Sharon's Plan: *I'm going to find a picture of a parrot and put it in a picture frame on my desk as a touchstone. I'm also going to start journaling about the courage to change.*

JOURNALING

Sharon's Journal: *3/15: Today I bought earrings that have green, red, and blue in them. I want to wear these to remind me of the parrot's wings. When I think of the parrot, my fear decreases, and saying or doing something for myself is so much easier. I was able to tell my friend Kathy how she hurt my feelings last week when she cancelled our hike, when it sounded like she was opting to take time with a different friend over me. I'm so glad I did. It let me find out how her other friend was having medical problems, and she was not just trading one playtime for another. I wouldn't have been able to do that before. Thank you, my heart.*

4/7: I made plans to fly to Mexico next month for a one-week immersion class in Spanish. I'm thrilled and scared. After a sleepless night, I told Steve I needed time to be alone and think about our relationship. I knew he'd be angry in his cold, distant way, but it's okay. It's all okay. I don't know exactly what I want, and it's okay. I'm feeling my wings, I'm feeling my mobility, and that feels very right.

EYES OPEN IMAGERY:
Cultivating an Awareness of Wholeness

We mold ourselves, often unconsciously, to the ways we think others see us. How our parents once expected us to behave has become an unwritten contract for how to receive love and approval, and how to belong. But what if you are not the person that is seen through your mother's eyes, or the one who is now defined by your partner's expectations? What if you are not even the person you think you are?!

- Make a list of eight to twelve qualities that are a good representation of how you are. For example, it might include things like being kind, honest, fearful, outgoing, discontented, and so on.

  Now list the opposite of each—being unkind, dishonest, courageous, quiet, content, and so on. Are you sure that this second list does not also describe you? Come up with two or three examples of how you have behaved in a given situation that would match the second list of qualities. Sift through your memories of a time when you have been unkind (if it is on your list) to yourself or another person. How did you act? What did you do or say? Now find a second example. And when was there a time that you have been dishonest? Did you ever neglect saying the whole truth to someone, even for "good reasons"? Continue until you have come up with several examples for the entire list.

- Create a collage of your "opposite" qualities, using pictures and phrases from magazines. When it is complete, get acquainted with this other you, this "shadow" self. Befriend this beautiful being who is discovering how to be in this strange and wonderful world.

- Now look in the mirror and see all of you: the kind and unkind you, the honest and dishonest you, the fearful and brave you. Let this being who is reflected back in the mirror be a living image. What do you see?

CHAPTER FIVE

GETTING TO THE HEART OF THE MATTER:
CLARIFYING YOUR CONCERNS

One step at a time is good walking.

CHINESE PROVERB

A DEVASTATING LIFE EVENT not only sends us into deep emotional pain, but it also creates upheaval with our beliefs about life and ourselves. Our most fundamental reference points shatter—who we thought we were and the anticipated direction of our life. Daily life can feel deeply disorienting when our usual comforts are no longer present.

For example, someone who has just received a life-threatening medical diagnosis will feel the impact of such news touching all aspects of his or her life. There are financial stresses with medical bills, changes in body image, questions about why this is happening, changes in relationships with family members and friends, living with the heightened sense of uncertainty, facing mortality fears, and so on. These multiple issues can easily become overwhelming, and it can be difficult to find a single word or phrase to start the guided imagery to find guidance and relief.

Multiple emotions are like a logjam on a river. They pile together and stop the flow. In forestry, the trick to freeing a logjam is to identify the one log that would best unlock the tangle of all the others and get it to shift. Similarly, it is valuable to identify the pivotal emotional concern in a crisis. Often by doing an imagery session on the core theme, the relief flows out to the other areas of life.

Here is a simple, six-step process that can help you identify your key emotional "log," bringing you to the heart of the matter.

Getting to the Heart of the Matter

1. Over the course of a week, make a list of the disturbing thoughts that are part of your crisis.

2. Rate the emotional intensity of each thought on a scale of 1 to 10, with 10 being the most intense.

3. Identify the three thoughts that come up most often.

4. Write the three thoughts in a single paragraph.

5. Look for a common thread in those three statements and reduce it to a single sentence.

6. Distill the sentence into a short word or phrase.

Let's look at how this process worked with Stan, who was devastated when he learned that his wife was having an affair.

"Ever since I discovered that Susie was having an affair with my best friend, I have been living with a barrage of feelings for months. I've been shocked, angry, and I had the deepest pain in my chest—I thought I was having a heart attack. I can't get out of the cycle of pain. I think it was the lying, the deceit, that stunned me the most. And they were spending time together in our home when I was at work! It makes me sick. I'm a fool. I'm overwhelmed, I can't sleep, and don't know where to begin."

I asked Stan to follow the six steps, beginning with recording the thoughts that go through his mind over the course of a week. He came up with a list and rated the intensity of the emotions that go with each aspect, putting an asterisk by the three thoughts that occurred most frequently.

STEPS 1, 2, AND 3

- I'm losing my marriage. (9)

- My kids will be damaged for life. (10)

- Susie was my best friend. How could she do this to me? (10*)

- My home is tainted. (8)

- The specialness of our marriage can never be restored. (9)

- I'll never trust another person. (9)

- I've been used. (7)

- I can't trust myself. I was so blind! (10*)

- I'm not good enough. She went for someone else. (10)

- My self-respect is gone. (8)

- I'm going to be in financial ruin. (7)

- I hate the person I love, and I hate myself for that. (9)

- I want to forgive and get over this, but I can't. (9)

- My dreams are shattered; my life is ruined. (10)

- A similar thing happened to me in my twenties. What's wrong with me? (8)

- This shouldn't be happening. I want out of this nightmare. Life sucks. God sucks. (10*)

In step 4, he grouped together his top three recurring statements that had been noted with an asterisk.

STEP 4

"Susie was my best friend, how could she do this to me? I can't trust myself. I was so blind! This shouldn't be happening. I want out of this nightmare. Life sucks. God sucks."

As he considered his condensed statement, he began to clarify a core theme. He rephrased it for step 5.

STEP 5

"Because I can't trust my ability to see what's going on around me, it makes life too frightening."

He then completed step 6, and distilled his statement into a phrase to use for the self-facilitation imagery session.

STEP 6

"I'm blind."

On the next pages is Stan's self-facilitated guided imagery journey to the wisdom of his heart.

Journey to the Wisdom of the Heart
SELF-FACILITATION WORKSHEET

1. WHAT DO YOU NEED GUIDANCE ABOUT? (ONE MINUTE)

Stan's Topic: *I'm blind.*

2. JOURNEY TO YOUR HEART BY TRAVELING INWARD (THREE TO FOUR MINUTES)

Stan's Journey: *I tried to sit quietly and do breathing exercises, but my body ached and my mind was racing. I finally stood up and did part of a kickboxing warmup that I know. There is a lunging and jabbing movement to the right and left. I put some muscle into it. I used a simple repetition and stayed with it. I felt much more calm after ten minutes and was then able to sit down and continue.*

3. DISCOVERING YOUR INNER SANCTUARY (THREE MINUTES)

Stan's Inner Sanctuary: *I'm in a cave at the edge of the ocean. It's a section of cliff that has been carved out by the waves over time. It's about seven or eight feet deep, maybe five feet tall—not high enough to stand up in. It's twilight, almost dark. The sky and water are gray. It's cool and moist inside the cave, and the smell of the sea is very strong but pleasant. I'm sitting cross-legged on the sand, and there are bits of shells and seaweed here and there. The walls of rock are embedded with chipped shells and pebbles. I'm looking out at the water. The waves look glassy. I feel very alive, and want to take time breathing in the sea air. It is refreshing. I feel the blood coursing through my body and I feel stronger than I have in a long time.*

Healing and Transformation through Self-Guided Imagery

4. BRINGING YOUR TOPIC TO HEART (ONE MINUTE)

Stan's Topic: *I'm blind.*

5. RECEIVING YOUR HEART'S MESSAGE (THREE TO FIVE MINUTES)

Stan's Heart's Message: *I silently ask my heart to come to my aid regarding my blindness. I sit quietly in the cave and notice a crab quickly moving sideways with it's back to me. At first I thought it was just part of the environment, but then I had the sense it was there for a reason. I just watched it, and it was very intent on picking through the bits of shell and seaweed, looking for food I think. It seemed as though it was completely unaware that I was there. Then it dawned on me, all at once. The crab was showing me myself. I get so absorbed at work and get into a survival mode of looking for the next customer that I don't even know what's around me. I see I've had my back turned to Susie, not realizing she's even there, especially when I bring work home, which has been a lot in the last year or two. When I realized this, the crab turned around and looked me right in the eyes. It was kind of strange, but it felt like a confirmation.*

6. THANKING YOUR HEART (TWO MINUTES)

Stan's Thanks: *Wow.*

DEEPENING YOUR UNDERSTANDING

Stan's Insights: *I thought a lot about the image of the crab and I was able to find other meanings in the symbol—the ways I have a protective shell around me, the ways I scavenge in my life because I'm afraid there won't be enough, and the ways I get crabby. I'm still upset about what Susie did, but I see for the first time how I have a part in creating the situation. I had thought I was the responsible, caring person and that she was the one who destroyed everything. I totally blamed her. I hadn't been open to believing that our marriage could survive this, but we are going to start couples counseling and see if we can sort through this. I don't know if we will stay together or not, but at least it seems like something we can start to talk about now.*

BRINGING YOUR HEART'S WISDOM INTO DAILY LIFE

Stan's Plan: *I am finding new goals and behaviors. First, I am setting a limit on my workday. When it is over, I'm going to make the transition final. I plan to take a run or go to the gym after work and really switch gears. Also, I'm practicing keeping my head up. I realize that when I'm going to the store or walking down the street, I'm oblivious to my environment. I'm actually going to notice the cashier behind the counter. It makes me wonder how I drive without getting in accidents. I'm in automatic pilot most of the time. With couples therapy, I'm going to hear what it has been like for Susie and not only focus on my pain. I realize I'm not blind if I look up.*

Stan came to see how he blinds himself by being absorbed in his thoughts and how looking up is one realistic remedy for restoring his vision. No longer a victim, he is empowered to make changes and create the life he wants. He is also learning more than he expected. Because he sees his part in contributing to the painful relationship dynamics, it creates new possibilities to repair his marriage that he didn't recognize were there.

Stan came up with sixteen stressful thoughts on his Getting to the Heart of the Matter list. Although he did have a significant breakthrough by exploring the core belief, "I'm blind," in his guided imagery session, continuing to gain his heart's perspective on *each* of his statements could yield amazing results. To the extent that his other beliefs go unexamined, perspectives such as "I'm not good enough," "My self-respect is gone," and "I've been used" may continue to influence his life in painful ways whether his marriage is repaired or he goes on with his life as a single father.

We explored earlier how crisis is an opportunity. And the opportunity for Stan and all of us when faced with suffering is to discover greater freedom and wisdom in our lives. Stan's crisis brought him insight into unconscious behaviors that he is in the process of changing. Whatever the outcome for his marriage, his life will be the richer for keeping his head up and being more present to whomever he is with.

When a crisis challenges our underlying beliefs, it is a chance to uproot negative patterns that have been shaping our lives for years. Stan notes in his list of stressful thoughts, "A similar thing happened to me in my twenties. What's wrong with me?" A few months later, he did a guided imagery journey on his recurring pattern of behavior. He identified the word *betrayed* in order to explore the patterns of infidelity that he has experienced in more than one relationship. Here is the first part of Stan's guided imagery worksheet:

Stan: *I found myself on a barren hill, wrapped in a gray wool blanket. There was a cold wind blowing. When I asked for my heart's aid on betrayal, images of former relationship partners appeared, and a steel, mechanical arm came out of my torso and clamped around them, pulling them toward me. I had the image of a heat-seeking missile. I realize that I didn't really get to know my partners as individuals, what they wanted or needed. There is a way they were objects to keep me warm. They were meant to be a salvation to keep me from living a cold and lonely life.*

If you met Stan at a party, you would see an attractive, fit man in his late forties. A conversation with him would reveal a very responsible family man, hard working, who loves his kids. And yet in hearing Stan's imagery journey on betrayal, it could seem as though he's cold, manipulative, and unloving. This seeming contradiction is there because we are getting to know Stan through his courageous unveiling of what Jung describes as a *shadow aspect* of the personality. Stan is seeing in himself the parts that do not surface easily in the conscious mind and that go against the values he identifies with and wants to live by.

Jung describes the shadow as the unconscious or hidden aspects of ourselves that the ego either has never realized or has repressed. Although these parts of us can often be disagreeable to the conscious mind, they are not evil by nature. Jung, in *Psychology and Religion*, states, "Everyone carries a shadow, and the less it is embodied in the individual's conscious life, the blacker and denser it is. At all counts, it forms an unconscious snag, thwarting our most well-meant intentions."

We are all eager to have others acknowledge the attractive parts we play in relationships, the ways we are generous, loving, and understanding. It is much more difficult for most of us to face our less virtuous traits, the times when we are closed-minded, reacting out of fear, demanding our neediness be met by another. But to the extent that our shadow remains underground, it has the power to disrupt our lives. Guided imagery gently brings these hidden parts into the compassionate and wise awareness of the heart, opening the way to truly live an authentic life.

TERESA: CULTURAL SHAME

*You can never go home again, but the truth is
you can never leave home, so it's all right.*

MAYA ANGELOU

IT STARTED OUT a day like most others. By 7:45 AM the financial district in San Francisco is humming with the usual rush of suits streaming toward office doors. Teresa is juggling her purse, Peet's coffee, and a black leather bag that holds reports for an 8:00 AM meeting with the CEO.

Having spent her early twenties as a barista, working in a bookstore, and in a range of temporary jobs, she is proud that she completed a BA degree in business administration from the state university, and landed a marketing job three years ago. Her position offers the opportunity of climbing a promising career ladder. At thirty-one, she now has an apartment in the city and a fun set of colleagues, and the position has afforded her this. She's on track.

As her heels click briskly on the pavement, her mind shuffles a rapid series of thoughts and images: "I'm not sure I'm happy with the report—damn, I should have changed the closing summary; there goes my raise. I hate this skirt—too tight. Ummm, hope Rob calls for plans this weekend;

I'll wear my blue dress. Jason is such a creep, so conceited. I've got to leave on time tonight to meet Mary."

A red light interrupts her pace, and she checks her watch. She crosses the street and rounds the corner, absorbed again with the agenda for the 8:00 meeting when she nearly trips over a homeless woman camped out in the first patch of morning sunlight. As she catches her balance, Teresa drops her coffee, splashing hot latte everywhere. With a mixture of annoyance and embarrassment, Teresa mops up what she can with a wad of tissues from her purse and whispers a terse apology. The way the homeless woman is muttering to herself, lost in her own head, is really disturbing. She leaves the woman a twenty-dollar bill. Teresa runs to make up for lost time or maybe for the relief of just getting away from that upsetting situation.

Riding up the office elevator, Teresa is still shaken. Her arms and legs are buzzing from the shock of almost falling. The image of the homeless woman's dark, vacant eyes keeps burning in her mind—so vivid it feels as though she was nose to nose for a moment, as though space contracted—weird. Thinking about how the homeless are usually mentally unstable creates a knot in her stomach. She's lucky; anything could have happened to her in that encounter.

Suddenly a memory from last summer erupts in her mind: It's 3:00 AM, and she can't go back to sleep. Frightening images paint themselves across her mind through the night. The rumor of upcoming lay-offs in the company puts everyone on edge. Would she still have her job tomorrow? She has no financial reserves. How would she get by? Where would she live?

The elevator doors glide open with a "ding!" that pops her back into the morning, and she steps into the bright foyer, quickly slipping those dark memories into a back pocket of her mind.

That night Teresa has a dream. It's one of those dreams that seems to last the whole night, cohesive and strong, the kind of dream that rolls through your psychic foundation, twisting hinges, tipping and scattering carefully placed objects, and leaving doors ajar.

It's dawn, and the dream images linger as she opens her eyes: a bear, a baby, a gaping wound. She tries to focus on her work schedule, using the items on her "to do" list like rocks she can throw at a pack of menacing dogs. She gets up to make coffee but feels the nocturnal apparitions following her into the kitchen. There's something going on, and she doesn't like this at all. She is shaky and nauseous. And she does what she hasn't done for three years at her job—she calls in sick.

A few days later Teresa shows up in my office with the distressing feelings and dream images refusing to let up. She has never done any kind of counseling or guided imagery. After she tells me briefly about her home and work life, we settle in and Teresa tells me her dream.

"I lift up the flap of a cloth doorway. It's canvas, like on a tent, but I think it is on a shack of some kind. And I see a baby, a little girl. I realize it's my baby, and it's barely alive. The baby has a gaping wound in her side and somehow I learn a bear has attacked her. The bear has eaten part of her internal organs. I'm not sure what—a liver or something."

As she tells the dream, it's clear from the welling up of tears that these images continue to have a strong hold on her. She presses down on the cushion of the chair with the heels of her hands, as though her arms have the job of keeping her from collapsing.

"At one point in the dream, I realize that I had known about this attack on my baby, but it was so shocking to me that I had blocked it out for some period of time, I don't know how long, and now I was aware of it again. This makes it all the more disturbing."

Teresa is wearing gray sweatpants and a pink T-shirt. With her hair pulled back in a ponytail, I'm getting to see a very different Teresa from the well-put-together businesswoman she's described herself as. Although she can't make sense of the dream, it is very consuming, and Terea feels an urgency to relieve the feelings it stirs up in her. She continues.

"I'm running through town, frantically, trying to get help. It's a small town with dirt streets, the way it might have been here one hundred years ago. I run into a small apothecary and ask for help for my baby, asking how to treat the wound. They give me pills that I'm supposed to take. I find a friend and tell him about the baby, but it's as if I'm invisible. He can't see me. That's how it ends."

Teresa tells me that last year she had suffered from insomnia to the point that it was interfering with her work. Her physician prescribed sleeping pills to take as needed. She was wondering about a connection between the pills in the dream and the pills on her bed stand. Was this a piece of the puzzle of what was happening to her?

I asked Teresa if she would like to revisit the dream through guided imagery, explaining how imagery can dialogue with the dream figures, offering an opening for the understanding and relief she's looking for. She immediately said yes.

"Which part of the dream imagery is the strongest?" I inquire.

It takes her no time at all to respond, "The wound. It's the gaping wound in my baby girl." She hugs her elbows with her hands, pressing her arms across her torso as though her stomach hurts. We agree to make the healing of her wounded baby the focal point of the guided imagery.

"Close your eyes," I begin, "and take a full breath in. As you exhale, feel relaxation flowing through your body from your head down to your feet."

Teresa takes to this quite naturally and has already entered the imagery state. "I'm standing in a shallow, warm river. When I breathe in I scoop up water with a bucket, and when I breathe out, I pour it over my head like a shower. The water is warm and has a green tint."

I am watching her body relax as she breathes and we continue with this very simple relaxation, perfect for Teresa, for the next several minutes before we continue.

When she is ready to go on, I invite her to let an image form of a safe place to explore the healing of her baby's wound.

Teresa is engaging like a veteran of imagery, already in her inner sanctuary. "I step out of the river and into a lush jungle. Green—it's all deep, rich green. I'm sitting with my back against a *nance* tree, *changugu*. The jungle is full of life, but it feels very safe."

Although I have no idea what a *changugu* might be like, it's clear that Teresa is surrounded by exactly what she needs.

I am surprised that Teresa has begun to speak with a hint of a Spanish accent that had not been present just moments before. It is an amazing transformation as her more recent experiences dissolve to reveal underlying layers of her life. The jungle seems to root her to an early life I know nothing about. We are poised together on the mystery of what will arise next in the imagery, and we continue.

"Does this feel like a good time and place to seek healing for your baby's wound?" I ask.

Teresa looks solemn and steady, the way some people snap into a very calm state in the midst of a disaster. It's the first time she speaks of the baby without being shaky and tense. She simply states, "I'm ready. My baby is here with me."

I am very moved by this brave, young woman, so ready to face her fears.

"Invite an image to form for the kind of healing that your baby needs," I prompt her. Although her eyes are closed, the concentration showing in her face suggests that she is focusing a short distance in front of her in the jungle.

Teresa responds. "An old woman approaches me. She has a face that has spent lots of time in the sun. She looks very kind and wise. A grandmother. I feel like I know her. She's short, and her body is square. Square shoulders and hips, square hands and feet. She is a medicine woman. And I trust her right away. It's obvious she knows what to do."

I ask Teresa if the medicine woman has a name.

Teresa pauses and slips effortlessly into her native tongue, Spanish. She asks the medicine woman what her name is.

"Tula," she translates for me. "Call me Tula."

It's clear that Teresa is very engaged in the guided imagery and that the exchange with Tula is now occurring in Spanish. Although I typically stay verbally connected with the person during the imagery journey, I'm aware that asking Teresa to translate for me as she goes could distract from her experience. I decide to keep my questions to a minimum, just enough exchange to track that she is getting what she needs.

When the session is complete and she opens her eyes, Teresa has a stillness about her, like that feeling the air gets at dusk when even the birds are quiet. When she describes her time with the medicine woman, Teresa's eyes are glassy, as though she is still seeing beyond the walls of this room and into Tula's face. Teresa describes her guided imagery journey.

"Tula brushes aside the leaves and twigs, creating a soft place on the jungle floor. She asks me to place the baby there. Tula then puts her hands on my baby's head and feet and closes her eyes. After a moment, she asks me to place my hands on my baby's head and feet. Tula then places her hands over mine. I can feel a warm energy flowing through my hands into the baby. It feels like golden honey. Tula is silently teaching me how to do this.

"Tula then tells me that I am to place my hands on my own heart and belly every night when I am in bed and feel the same golden honey flowing in me before I go to sleep. She says to pay close attention to the honey, the kind of attention I would need if I wanted to watch a flower blossom open—very slow and very attentive.

"I ask Tula about the bear, and why the baby was attacked. Tula tells me very kindly and firmly that this is not the time for that answer. This is a healing time.

"Tula is patient with all my questions. I tell her that the nighttime practice makes sense to me, but I wonder about what to do during the day, especially at work. Tula tells me to bind the baby to myself. 'Don't run. Don't jostle her. Don't leave her on the bus.' She tells me to take the same care as if I were carrying an egg in my hand through the day.

"When it becomes clear that our time together is drawing to a close, Tula puts her hands on my temples. It feels like she is checking for a fever from my inner body the way a parent presses a child's forehead to check temperature. Tula then spits into the earth and makes a paste that she places on my forehead with her thumb. With kindness pouring from her eyes, she says, *'Hija se te olvidan los pies, no olvides tus raices.'* 'Even the mud feels like I am anointed with honey.'"

I was curious about Tula's last statement, "Don't forget your feet, daughter. Don't forget where you are from." I asked Teresa if she knows what Tula is communicating to her.

Teresa nodded. After a long pause, she tells me that her father is deceased and that her mother and most of her siblings live in Mexico. Teresa is ashamed of the poverty that she came from, and it continues to be the environment most of her family lives in. Although she sends her mother money every month, Teresa has been diligent about erasing any trace of an accent and speaking impeccable English. She wouldn't consider dating a Latino or be caught dead eating in a taqueria. She has tried to seal off her childhood as a way to create a radically different life for herself here. Although she keeps her feelings buried much of the time, every so often she is very torn about the ways she has cut herself off from the family ties that are such a deep part of her cultural heritage. Although she feels good about her career successes, she also feels divided, dishonest, and deeply guilty.

"Tula showed me that my roots are beautiful, and I did feel so at peace on the land in my guided imagery. There was a deep 'at home' restfulness that I have not felt in years."

I feel such a deep tenderness for Teresa and am so glad she is willing to share her story with me. "What would you like to do with the messages from Tula?" I inquire.

"Oh," Teresa responds quickly, "I am so grateful to her. I am going to do those evening exercises and be with my baby girl during the day, too. Tula told me she is always available to me and asked me to come back soon. I very much would like to do that."

Teresa and I met several times over the next year, and she was also able to enter the imagery at home quite easily. So far, Tula has remained consistent that it is still not the time for Teresa to know more about the bear that attacked her baby. As so often occurs with guided imagery, we enter the session with one expectation and come out of it with something even richer than we could have anticipated. Teresa describes how doing the guided imagery feels like opening up and restoring rooms of a house that have been boarded up and filled with dust. Her eyes are taking on a kindness that looks the way I have imagined Tula's eyes.

Six months after our initial meeting, Teresa tells me she is volunteering one night a week as an English tutor to immigrant children. If Tula could whisper in my ear as she looks at Teresa through my eyes for a moment she might say: *Hija, estas regresando maravillosamente a tus raices.* Daughter, you are coming home to yourself so beautifully.

EYES OPEN IMAGERY:
Cultivating an Awareness of Roots

Feeling our roots goes to the question "Who am I?" Let's start exploring this question close to home. Who are you as the child of your parents and as a sibling? Are you a mother or a father yourself, an aunt or an uncle, a first cousin, second cousin, third cousin, fourth cousin? Where does your family end?

Like an intricate web, the threads of blood relations connect outward in all directions. We may not know all the people by name or have the information to trace the unbroken lineage. We may not have categories to name the living links that spread exponentially. But where does it actually stop? Where does the line between family and nonfamily exist? Can you be absolutely sure that a stranger passing you on the sidewalk is not actually related to you?

- See the next three people that you come into contact with, whether known or unknown to you, as a living image of the web of family.

- Find a book or magazine with photographs of people from around the world. Everyone is so unique, so fascinating. Notice the different features, the range of hair texture and colors, shades of skin tones, body shapes and sizes.

The river of life within our bodies is not divided by color, as is evident in any blood bank. Know that one of the people in the magazine, who looks nothing like you and lives so radically differently from you, could share his blood with you through a transfusion, if the medical need arose, and save your life. Choose one of the people in the photographs and embrace him as a living image of your blood brother or blood sister.

- We live in a universe that has a hundred billion galaxies—a hundred billion and counting. It is estimated that there are five million to one hundred million species on this planet. We live in a mysterious place where on the one hand, we are completely unique. There is only one of you on the entire planet. And yet the same pure substance, the particles and life force that brings everything into existence, unites us all. This miraculous place is our home.

    No one else gets to be you. Let yourself shine. *Be* the living image of your glorious one-of-a-kind and universal you.

CHAPTER SIX

WAYS TO
TRAVEL INWARD

*Out beyond ideas of wrongdoing and rightdoing
there is a field. I'll meet you there.*

JALAL AD-DIN RUMI

TRAVELING INWARD can be the most challenging part of the
guided imagery process, especially if you are seeking guidance for a distressing situation. You may ask, "How can I possibly sit still and breathe
'peace' when my thoughts keep circling time and again into painful
images, my heart is aching, and I'm seized by fear that makes me want
to jump out of my skin?" Know that it is possible to shift into a relaxed
state, with a little time, the right tools, and a clear intention.

One person can experience a situation as stressful that to another is
enjoyable. A big party may be a great way for an extrovert to clear out
stress, but the same party can increase stress for some introverts. Just
as stress is relative, so too the easiest way to relax varies from person
to person. You may find that the breathing exercise included in the Self-
Facilitation Worksheet is an effective way for you to relax and enter your
inner sanctuary. But if this is not the case, you are invited to try other
exercises in this chapter and find the best fit for you. There are a variety
of proven, reliable tools for traveling inward to your heart's wisdom.

When we are in crisis, it signals our body's survival mechanisms, and we have the same physiological response that our human relatives have had for 25,000 to 40,000 years. When there is anything that we perceive as a threat, whether fighting a mammoth or facing a financial crisis, the same cascade of chemicals is released into the body, creating the fight-or-flight stress response and preparing us for action. Our sympathetic nervous system is activated, resulting in an increase in heart rate and blood pressure, quick shallow breathing, a thickening of the blood, and the release of adrenaline and other stress hormones, to name just a few of the changes. And the recurring painful images in our minds perpetuate the stress response by feeding the ongoing sense of threat. This is often where we are starting when we sit down to travel inward.

The good news is that we can intentionally trigger a calming response and restore equilibrium to our bodies, minds, and emotions by activating a different physiological response through the parasympathetic nervous system, or network. This chapter will teach a variety of methods for creating the relaxation response that arises from that network. This is the first step to traveling inward. And if you are already relatively calm, these exercises can deepen your inner repose.

All of the practices in this chapter share the focus of breaking the cycle of our incessant thinking that perpetuates the stress response. Because our compulsive thinking is so prevalent, almost everyone considers it "normal." But the constant cycling of worries and judgments fuels our ongoing distress. These habitual thoughts are a block to accessing our heart's inner wisdom. When we shift awareness out of our thoughts, we create an open path straight to our wise hearts.

The exercises in this chapter become more effective with practice and will also develop your power of concentration. For example, if you try the first breathing exercise, you are asked to feel how the movement of your breath creates an expansion and contraction in your belly. Watching your breath may be fairly easy for the first breath, the second breath, but before you know it, there comes a point when you realize that your mind has drifted back to your disturbing thoughts and images. This is completely normal. When this happens, and it will, you simply redirect your focus to your breath. Redirecting your attention strengthens your concentration and is one of the benefits of this practice.

Like developing any new skill, the ability to concentrate gets easier with practice. If you are learning to play the piano, placing your fingers in the position to practice scales can initially feel awkward and unnatural. Maybe your fingers get fatigued or cramp up after a few minutes. These early, frustrating moments at the piano can feel far away from your inspiration to play music. You might even think that you have no natural talent. But with time, your body becomes comfortable with the new finger positions. You develop familiar motor skills, strengthening particular muscle groups. What once seemed so effortful and awkward becomes second nature. The same is true with these exercises for traveling inward.

Because cultivating concentration takes practice, it is important to bring a quality of kindness and patience toward yourself. Remember, you are evoking relaxation, and to insert self-criticism as you practice can tip the scale in the opposite direction. When we notice we have drifted from the focus on our breath, it is easy to believe we are failing at the exercise (out, damned thought!). But the opposite is actually true. Each time we redirect our attention, we are succeeding at strengthening our concentration.

As we cultivate the relaxation response, most of us will benefit from the well-documented effects, such as a slower heart rate and a decrease in blood pressure. But it is important to fine-tune these practices to fit your unique circumstances. For example, if you are currently taking medication for your heart or if you are prone to very low blood pressure, you will want to keep any changes within a range that is optimal for you. Discussing this with your medical practitioner is an important way to understand and monitor the physiological changes that these powerful practices can have.

As you try out the exercises, find a comfortable setting where you can arrange to be undisturbed by telephone calls or visitors. Remember that the relaxation practices for traveling inward continue for a minimum of three minutes or until you feel calm and relaxed.

The basic relaxation practice below blends several of the elements we will explore in greater detail in this chapter, including breathwork, progressive relaxation, witnessing thoughts, and focusing words or mantras. It is a good foundational practice. A free downloadable MP3 of this relaxation practice is available at www.LeslieDavenport.com. Reading these scripts aloud with a friend is also a lovely way of doing the work. You can also record your own voice, setting the pace that is ideal for you.

Basic Relaxation Practice: Traveling Inward

Sit or recline in a comfortable position, letting your body be well supported. Let your body really release into the support. Just let go and relax. Now turn your thoughts for just a moment toward the last couple of hours—the activities, conversations, and things you have experienced. Take a snapshot of that time; recognize it as part of your past. Let the snapshot drift away from you, and make more room for this moment, now. Turn your thoughts for just a moment to the things you anticipate doing later today. Take a snapshot of that time; recognize it as part of your future. Let the picture drift away from you, and make more room for this precious moment, now. As you breathe, let go of anything that doesn't serve you in this moment.

This moment, which is fresh and uncluttered, has never been lived before. Feel the clear spaciousness of this present moment. Let the natural quality of peace ride on your breath. As you take a full breath in, feel the spaciousness, and silently say the word *clarity*. When you breathe out, silently say the word *peace* as you continue to relax even more deeply. Breath in clarity, breath out peace. In, clarity; out, peace.

On the next in-breath, let the fresh, clear feeling rise up to the top of your head. As you breathe out, let peacefulness flow over your scalp and forehead. Now breathe clarity into your mind. As you breathe out, experience the peace that is always present beyond thoughts. Breathe fresh clarity into your eyes, your face. As you exhale, let your eyes rest and your face relax. Notice your jaw in particular, allowing it to be slack and loose as you exhale.

Let the next breath bring fresh energy into your throat, open and clear. On the out-breath, feel peacefulness flowing into your neck, shoulders, and upper back. Feel your muscles softening in response. Let the flow of relaxation travel into your arms, hands, and fingers. Notice the subtle sensations that arise. Do they feel warm or tingling or light? Just notice, and enjoy.

Now bring your awareness and breath into your torso. Breathe freshness and clarity into your heart. Discover the peacefulness that abides there as you breathe out. Breathe fresh energy into all the vital organs, allowing them to feel natural, comfortable, and relaxed as you breathe out. Breathe in, clarity; breathe out, peace.

Let your breath and awareness continue into your hips. Feel your belly receiving your breath, rising on the inhalation, and settling on the exhalation, fresh and peaceful. Let the fresh energy and peaceful feelings flow into your legs, all the way to your feet and toes. Let the soles of your feet relax, the way they might feel on warm sand, soft grass, or a smooth river stone.

Now feel your whole body, a three-dimensional sensation, vibrant and peaceful. Breathing in, your whole body, clear. Breathing out, your whole body, peaceful. Every breath soothing. Every breath a blessing. Breathing in, your whole being, clear. Breathing out, your whole being, peaceful.

BREATHING

Deep breathing is the fastest way to activate the parasympathetic nervous system, and it can occur in a matter of seconds. Breath practices are not only relaxing but also restorative because oxygen levels increase, fueling your natural vitality. Breathwork is also an invaluable tool for balancing and stabilizing the mind and emotions.

Recent research by Patricia Gerbarg, MD, and Richard Brown, MD, in *The Journal of Family Practice* and *Current Psychiatry*, documents how forms of breathwork have been shown to significantly relieve symptoms of trauma in survivors of war, terrorism, and natural disasters. In one study, more than one thousand residents of New York participated in free yoga breathing classes two weeks after the September 11, World Trade Center attack. The research indicated that the common effects of trauma, such as anxiety, insomnia, depression, and hyperarousal, rapidly improved and had lasting positive impact with these breath-focused interventions. Knowing of the success of breathwork with trauma, it's easy to imagine the benefits with the less severe life stressors we face much of the time.

If you have respiratory problems, emphasize the quality of *ease* rather than the depth of your breathing. Deeper breathing may come more gradually as you pay attention to the edges of your comfort and gently allow them to expand.

Abdominal Breathing The abdominal breathing exercise presented here covers the foundation of good breath practice. If abdominal breathing is new to you, I suggest that you do this lying on your back the first few times. Get comfortable. You can bend your knees with a pillow placed under them, which is so relaxing for the lower back. It is also possible to do this breathing exercise in a sitting position.

If you observe an infant, you will see how her belly moves when she breathes. This also occurs when adults sleep. With an in-breath, the abdomen naturally rises, and it recedes on the exhalation. Because of the stress and muscle tension many of us accumulate, we sometimes lose this natural way of breathing. It is easy and very beneficial to relearn this, but it takes time to establish new habits.

Lie on your back and close your eyes. Place your right palm so that it rests lightly on your belly, below your navel. Inhale in a way that lets you feel your abdomen rising. The placement of your hand will help you sense this area of your body and the movement of the breath. When you exhale, feel your belly receding. At the end of the exhalation, squeeze your abdominal muscles, pushing the last bit of air out of your lungs. This will naturally lead to a deep inhalation on the next breath. Continue hollowing out the belly at the end of the first five out-breaths. Following the first five cycles of the breath, continue with abdominal breathing but let your breath find its own natural rhythm, without the additional squeezing motion.

Let your mental concentration track the rise and release of your belly, being attentive to each in-breath and each out-breath. You may find that your breathing gradually becoming deeper and slower. Watch each part of the breath the way you would watch the ebb and flow of the tides at the ocean. If your mind wanders to other thoughts, bring your attention back to your breath each time you notice it has drifted. Simply continue this for three minutes or until you are deeply relaxed.

Nose and Mouth Breathing Follow the same instructions for abdominal breathing, but for the first five breaths, inhale through your nose and exhale through your mouth, squeezing out all remaining air at the end of the exhalation by pulling in your belly. Have your lips pursed as though you were going to blow out a candle, making a sustained audible sound. It will sound similar to wind in the trees.

Three-Part Breathing (Dirgha Pranayama) The most developed of breath practices come from the yogic traditions and are known as *pranayama*. Dating back close to eight thousand years, *prana* is a Sanskrit word with a variety of meanings, including breath, life force, energy, vitality, and even spirit or soul. *Yama* translates as "restraint," and in this case refers to control of the breath.

The three-part breath is considered a complete breath in the yogic practice and builds upon the foundation of abdominal breathing. It is especially good for oxygenating the blood.

As with abdominal breathing, I would suggest that you try it the first few times lying down before doing it as a sitting practice. Breathe through the nose for both the in- and the out-breath. As with abdominal breathing, let your mental concentration be on tracking the path of each breath through the body, returning to your breath as soon as you notice a distraction.

As you begin to inhale, let your belly rise as it fills with air. As you continue to draw in breath, feel you midbody, your lower rib cage, also expanding. Toward the end of the in-breath, let the breath continue filling your torso, all the way to an expansion in the upper chest, under the collarbones. Reverse the process on the exhalation, letting the breath drain first from the upper chest, then feeling the release of the rib cage, and ending with the belly receding. Eventually you will feel each section expanding and releasing in one smooth flow.

We tend to focus on movement in the front part of our body as we draw in breath. Notice that there is also a subtle expansion that occurs in the side and back of our torso. The same is true as the breath rises into the upper chest. It may help to picture your lungs as large balloons that fill in all directions.

Cleansing Breath (Nadi Shodhana) Also from the yogic tradition, this breath practice is said to balance out the system by regulating the energy pathways that run through the right and left parts of the body.

Bring your right hand up to your face and lightly place your ring finger and pinky on the left side of your nose. Place your thumb lightly on the right side of your nostril. Gently close the left nostril by pressing it with your ring finger and pinky. As you do this, take a slow full inhalation through the right nostril.

When you have taken in a full breath, place your thumb against your right nostril and release the left, fully exhaling through the left side.

Now inhale through the left, close it, and exhale through the right.

This sequence marks one full breath cycle.

Start with this alternating breathing for about ten cycles and then let your breath shift into abdominal breathing for the remaining time. As with all the breath practices described thus far, keep your attention on the awareness of the path of your breath.

Counting the Breath This exercise can be added to any of the breath practices described above. Adding counts to the breath can be helpful in focusing the mind. It also regulates the rhythm of the breath, which has a balancing effect on the body-mind-spirit.

As you inhale, silently count 1–2–3–4–5, setting the pace that matches a full, comfortable breath. Use the same pace as you exhale: 1–2–3–4–5.

Adding a Color You can also picture a color infusing your breath as part of any breath practice. The best way to select which color to use is to try them out and pay attention to how you feel, choosing the one that is a good fit in the moment.

Imagine a color as a fine mist that fills your body, mind, and energy field. As you breathe in, imagine a warm color, taking time to feel each one: red . . . rose . . . orange . . . peach . . . bold and soft yellows. . . . Notice how each color makes you feel. Now try out cooling colors: purple . . . lavender . . . deep and light blues . . . emerald and spring greens. . . . Return to the color that feels the best right now. Breathe it in, letting the colorful mist fill all the levels and dimensions of who you are. Breathe it out, noticing how far it travels.

PROGRESSIVE RELAXATION

Body Scan with Muscular Release The basic relaxation script presented earlier gives a good example of a body scan. The primary theme is to heighten your attention to your body sensations in the moment and replace areas of muscular constriction with softness. Here is another example of a body scan, this one asking you to actively engage the muscle groups rather than prompting relaxation only through awareness and breath.

As you inhale through your nose, hold tightly each of the positions described below for five counts. Then release your breath and the posture on an exhalation through your mouth, making an audible sigh.

- Raise your eyebrows as high as you can, creating horizontal creases in your forehead. (Hold for five counts and then release.)

- Squeeze your eyebrows tightly together, creating vertical creases in your forehead. (Continue with five counts for each area.)

- Pinch your eyes and mouth as close to your nose as you can—a whole face pucker.

- Open your eyes, your mouth, and your face as wide as you can, sticking your tongue out as far as it will go.

- Raise your shoulders as high as you can up toward your ears.

- Roll your shoulders forward, curling them as close to your sternum as possible.

- Press your shoulders back, feeling your shoulder blades slide together.

- Bend your elbows and tighten your hands into fists, squeezing your entire upper and lower arms.

- Tighten your stomach, making it as hard as you can.

- Contract your hips, tightening your buttocks.

- Flex your feet, tightening your thighs and calves, and curl your toes.

- Tighten your entire body, contracting it toward your waist from both directions, folding in your arms and legs. Repeat the whole body contraction and release three times.

Just relax now, palms facing upward, and feel the subtle quality of relaxation flowing outward through your arms and legs and through your torso from the soles of your feet to the crown of your head.

Autogenic Training Autogenic training was developed in the 1930s by the German psychiatrist Johannes Schultz. He coauthored a series of books with Wolfgang Luthe, including *Autogenic Training: A Psychophysiologic Approach in Psychotherapy*, which describe the methods and benefits of this technique. It shares similarities with the body scan, but it follows a prescribed set of directions, emphasizing a feeling of warmth and heaviness throughout the body. I have condensed and modified the autogenic exercises here from their original form, which are usually taught in phases over a three-month period.

Lie comfortably on your back and close your eyes. Take three full and complete breaths.

The phrases below are spoken internally and coordinated with the breath cycle.

Say the first part of the phrase (prior to the dash) silently as you inhale. As you breathe out, internally say the second half of the phrase.

My arms and legs are—heavy and warm. *Repeat three times.*

My heartbeat and breathing are—calm and steady.
Repeat three times.

My stomach is—soft and warm. *Repeat three times.*

My forehead is—cool. *Repeat three times.*

I feel—supremely calm. *Repeat three times.*

WATCHING YOUR THOUGHTS

About fifteen years ago, I saw a sweet little reminder of truth just above the tailpipe of a Pontiac in Berkeley. The bumper sticker read, "Don't Believe Everything You Think." I love how truth can be found everywhere, even on a strip of rusted chrome.

As we explore relaxation and the stress response, we see how the mind, body, and emotions are interconnected. The way they influence each other is a classic chicken-and-the-egg question. We can relax the physical body with breathing and a body scan and notice how our mind also quiets in response. Or we can help settle our thoughts and see how the body and emotions also release. The next two exercises initiate relaxation by working with thoughts.

Here is the key to how these thought-based relaxation practices work: rather than thinking a thought, become aware that you are thinking a thought. In other words, you step back from full engagement with the content of your thought and rather become an observer of your thought.

The essence of the practice is to just notice your thoughts rather than judge them (or judge yourself for thinking them), push them away, or engage with them. This begins to loosen the grip of compulsive thinking.

The Witness Take three full, slow breaths, and relax.

Simply sit quietly and pay attention to any voices in your head. The voices may comment about physical discomfort, recall a memory, bring up a fear, or engage in a plan. Become aware of the part of you that is noticing your thoughts. This part is the witness. Mentally step back from your thoughts so that your witness can simply watch thoughts come and go. Whenever you find yourself thinking your thoughts rather than wit-nessing them, that is the cue to step back again and simply watch your thoughts. Continue to repeat this process of disengaging from thoughts and returning to the witness for a minimum of three minutes. Rest in the space between the thoughts.

The Skylike Mind Sit comfortably and take three full breaths.

Bring your awareness to your mind and sense how it is vast and spacious, like a sky. Can you feel the edges of your mind? How far does it reach? Like a sky, feel your mind as clear, open, and fresh.

When a thought enters the sky of your mind, consider that thought to be like a bird that flies though the sky. During this time, consider each thought equally, whether it is a big fear or a little detail—it's just another kind of bird. Now it's here; now it's gone. Watch each one move through the sky. Be present in your vast, clear, skylike mind.

RHYTHM

Drumming Life expresses itself rhythmically, through the orbit of atoms, the beat of our hearts, the cadence of footsteps, the ebb and flow of tides, the turning of the seasons, and the expansion and contraction of the universe.

You do not need any special training to use drumming for a cen-tering relaxation. You do not even need a drum! Our bodies are great percussion instruments. Simply listen deeply to a rhythm, and allow yourself to join in by clapping your hands against your thighs and tap-ping your feet. The more you let yourself join the beat without concern for the right way to do it, the more the rhythm can carry you into your own heart of healing.

Here are four recordings that are wonderful resources to use for this rhythmic approach to relaxing and traveling inward:

- *Mystic Vision: Music that Unleashes the Human Heart*, Kokomon Clottey

- *Totem*, Gabrielle Roth and the Mirrors

- *Planet Drum*, Mickey Hart

- *Healing Session*, Babatunde Olatunji

Put on one of the CDs and sit upright in a chair with your hands resting on your thighs and your feet on the floor. Listen deeply with your whole body and let your hands and feet join the rhythm. Surrender to the beat and enjoy.

MOVEMENT

If your tried the drumming meditation, you may have found that joining with the rhythm pulled you up onto your feet and got you moving around the room! Gabrielle Roth in her book on dancing as a spiritual path, *Sweat Your Prayers*, mentions an old Sufi saying that goes, "God respects us when we work, but loves us when we dance." Many people find that an active meditation with movement or music is a more natural way to travel inward than a sitting meditation.

Natural Dance This approach is simple, and the most challenging part is to let it remain uncomplicated. Our bodies already know how to move expressively. It's simply a matter of not letting our concerns about a right way to do it get in the way of a spontaneous movement exploration.

Our bodies have a natural, rich movement language. You may find that your movements are small and subtle or expansive and grand. You may find yourself stretching upward or sinking low and connecting with the ground. Your movements may originate from deep in your belly or from your pinky finger. You may find yourself flailing, rocking, pausing, shaking, bouncing, or sliding. Whether you are moving lyrically or percussively, slowly or quickly, or in waves, lines, or spirals, let your body lead the way.

Pick music that you really enjoy, preferably with few past associations, or that goes with prescribed dance steps. The style can be anything that (literally) moves you—classical, percussion, contemporary, chants, world music. . . .

There are many lovely lyrical selections in the CD series in the Windham Hill collection and on Enya's *Paint the Sky with Stars.* The CD series by Gabrielle Roth and the Mirrors has a variety of musical forms that evoke a range of movement qualities.

Spontaneous Movement Clear the floor, let go, and move!

Walking Meditation There are a variety of structured movement meditations. Yoga, from the Hindu lineage, and tai chi chuan and qigong from traditional Chinese medicine, are some of the best known and most highly developed. Although these movement forms are quite complex, you can get a taste of a structured movement meditation through the Buddhist practice of a walking meditation.

Begin a slow, ordinary walk, either indoors or outdoors on a level surface. Let your arms be relaxed, with your hands clasped in front of you and resting against your belly. Lower your eyes toward the ground a couple feet in front of you, and relax your body.

The focus of this practice is to bring attention to the experience of your feet as you walk, noticing the actions of raising, lifting, pushing, dropping, touching, and pressing. Bring your attention to the sole of each foot as it cycles through each step, making contact with the space and the ground. When your focus drifts into thinking, bring your attention back to mindful walking.

SOUND

All of the practices for turning inward move our attention out of the thinking mind and into another mode of perception. Deep listening, becoming absorbed in sound, is a powerful way to be released from the grip of compulsive thinking. Although the meditative and healing effects of sound have been a part of indigenous cultures and spiritual traditions for centuries, modern research is helping usher that ancient wisdom into contemporary settings.

Mitchell Gaynor, MD, an oncologist at the Strang Cancer Prevention Center in New York uses Tibetan bowls and chanting as part of treating cancer patients. Gaynor, in his book *The Healing Power of Sound: Recovery from Life-Threatening Illness Using Sound, Voice, and Music*, states, "If we accept that sound is vibration and we know that vibration touches every part of our physical being, then we understand that sound is not 'heard' only through our ears but through every cell in our body." In a blind study, Gaynor's research showed that chemotherapy patients who used the sound therapy throughout their treatment had a 50 percent shorter recover time. At St. Agnes Hospital in Baltimore, music therapy has been incorporated into the cardiology unit. Raymond Bahr, MD, the director of coronary care, reports in *Spirituality and Health* magazine that "half an hour of music produces the same effect as 10 milligrams of Valium."

With the power of music having this level of impact, I invite you to experiment using music to soothe the savage beast of your mind.

Music This practice is about deep listening. The best music for this purpose is instrumental music, because words can stimulate the language area of the mind and engage the thinking process. Even Western classical music has its drawbacks, because the dynamic range can be emotionally evocative, and the aim here is for a peaceful state that settles the emotional tugs and pulls. Here are a few suggestions for musical selections that work well for traveling inward:

- *Tibetan Singing Bowls*, Music for Deep Meditation

- *Thursday Afternoon*, Brian Eno

- *In Unity*, Tim Wheater and David Lord

Sit comfortably, take a few full breaths, and listen deeply.

Ambient Sound We are in an ocean of sound, from the squawking of crows to the hum of a refrigerator, the distant swish of a passing car, or the hushed rustling of leaves. This practice is simply to be aware of sounds without adding mental commentary. For example, you may hear the sound of a neighbor's lawn mower, and your thoughts could kick in with, "I need to get Billy to pull weeds this weekend." Or the heater clicks on, and you start to worry about the utility bill. If you leave the direct experience of sounds and begin thinking, choose to let go of the thoughts and return to the pure experience of listening.

Listen. Notice what you are hearing.

Mantra This practice invites you to participate in making music by adding your voice. The art and science of mantra, speaking/chanting a divine word or phrase, is thousands of years old. As with any practice with such a long road through time, there are volumes of meaning and interpretation for the practice. Perhaps the most universally known mantra, Om, has an entire book within the Hindu scriptures attempting to define the meaning of those two letters.

You are invited to step into the essence of mantra practice by bringing to it a meditative or prayerful intention. Some authorities say that it is unnecessary to understand the translation of a mantra, because the majority of the benefits are derived from the vibrational effect of the sound rather than through the meaning.

There is a sing-along Om CD that is a very simple way to experience this ancient chanting practice: *Chanting Om*, Music for Deep Meditation. Simply add your voice to the chorus of voices that repeat the single tone and word on the CD.

It doesn't require learning Sanskrit to use mantra practice for traveling inward. There are inspired songs found in all sorts of unexpected places. Try this urban invocation by Leonard Cohen: *If It Be Your Will.*

Set the repeat play and listen for at least three minutes. You can either learn the lyrics or simply hum along.

There are a variety of romantic ballads that can transport us to a meditative state if we hold that the love being described is divine Love. Try listening to (and sing along or hum with) Cyndi Lauper's version of *At Last* as a song to your deepest self. Once you have heard this familiar song in a new way, you may be surprised to find how many songs can easily translate into a contemporary hymn.

The Buddhist tradition tells us that there are more than ten thousand dharma doors, or entryways to the Truth of life and ourselves. The practices presented here are just a few of the ways you may discover a clear path to your own heart. Let us now cross the threshold and explore the beautiful terrain of our hearts.

TERRANCE: DIABETES

All the art of living lies in a fine mingling
of letting go and holding on.

HENRY ELLIS

ON WHITE CONSTRUCTION PAPER, he carefully draws a series of simple diamond shapes, slowing descending in a vertical line down the center of the page. There is a brilliant blue one, a bold crimson, a deep emerald, each with a slight variation in the jewel-like design. Hunched over the paper, he draws with such focused intensity, each line distinct and deliberate, as though the Fates are relying on his completion of the task.

It is Terrance's third time attending the Art and Imagery Wellness support group, and no one knows much about him except that he wears a patch over one eye and walks with difficulty, requiring a cane. He looks like a modern-day pirate plucked by the collar of his Hawaiian shirt from Venice Beach and deposited at the door. With a muted flamboyance, he has the look of a millionaire sculptor who keeps a fortune tucked under his mattress.

As in the previous meetings, he is sullen and withdrawn, his hands propped on top of his cane, head lowered, peering out from beneath the rim of a sport's cap. Periodically he sends out a glance that growls, which successfully discourages the other group members from interacting much with him.

We start each meeting with a group guided imagery meditation, then take time to draw or write, and end with conversation. On this day, Terrance lets us see a glimpse of who lives behind the patch.

"Close your eyes and take a few, full clearing breaths. As you exhale, release whatever activities have been a part of your morning prior to coming here. Let the subtle sounds of this environment come to your ears as you become even more present to this moment." We continue with progressive relaxation and breathwork for the next ten minutes and then transition into the imagery. "Allow an image to form for a healing moment in your life. It could be a simple interaction with a friend, a time alone in nature, or any experience that put you in touch with your own sense of wholeness." I continue to point their attention to the colors, textures, sounds, and feelings of their experience to vivify the healing qualities. As the guided imagery comes to a close, we take fifteen minutes in silence to write or draw about it.

Several people share their drawings, but everyone's eyes keep darting to steal glances at the intense man who has yet to speak. Overcome by curiosity, one of the more bold members of the circle asks Terrance about his picture. As he begins to talk, it isn't long before his edginess and the group's wariness both fall away, and a tender space opens in the circle.

"It wasn't the first time that that my wife Claire had to call 911," he says while keeping his eyes turned down toward the table.

With thirty-five years of shared experience of progressive medical problems from diabetes as well as a heart condition, this couple had established a fairly regular rhythm of doctor's visits and medical procedures, punctuated by emergencies. We learned that one evening about four months ago, Terrance and Claire had finished dinner when his insulin levels became unstable. Combined with surfacing side effects from a new heart medication, his blood pressure began to plummet. He was efficiently bustled into an ambulance with the customary array of monitors and IV fluids. Terrance continues with a dry report of the events that night when he abruptly pauses. His face softens and his eyes tear up.

Terrance speaks of an experience that night that has continued to haunt him in a beautiful and perplexing way.

It begins in the ambulance with the sounds of the sirens, traffic, and medical conversations fading into silence while his eyes focus on the white ceiling quickly becoming diffuse with a soft light. Time dissipates. He is alone, caught in a space between worlds. And he is suffocating. He describes an overpowering visceral desperation, and the voice of his body tells him that death is imminent. Then there is a merciful surprise.

"I look up into an unfamiliar space and see a shimmering jewel. It is the most beautiful thing I have ever seen. It is alive. Then it drops down and enters me, becoming one breath. It is sublime. In a moment, another one appears, unique, different from the last one, but just as overwhelmingly beautiful. It also enters me as one breath. I don't know whether another will appear."

But the jewels did continue to arrive that night, radiant, mysterious, and generous, one breath at a time.

He points to the first diamond he drew. "I can't describe the precious gift I felt; each breath a gift from Life itself, the gift of Life itself. And I do know that each breath is just as precious right now."

The air stills, and we are bathed in the elegant beauty that spills from this gruff man.

By reentering his profound experience through guided imagery and sharing it with the group, he is now ready for the impact from that occurrence, which has been incubating for months, to be fully born.

Over the next several months we heard more about the Terrance who had lived much of his life finding pride in a take the bull by the horns approach to life's challenges. But the impact of that night in the ambulance had put a crack in the hard shield of his personality, and the group had the beautiful opportunity of watching it open even further over the next year.

We also saw the unfortunate progression of his disease, leading to the amputation of one leg and eventually the other one, too. And although his body was growing smaller right before our eyes, his heart and spirit were growing larger.

It is said that when we are witnessed, we can't go back to our previous ways, and when we witness another, we are changed forever. The group's witnessing of Terrance's unfolding was a gift that flowed in all directions. The profound gift he received from that life-altering experience also became a gift to the group. And the group's deep appreciation and natural affection for him touched him deeply. Terrance's life journey was enhanced in a way that would not have occurred in isolation. And the members of the group were also transformed through the encounters.

Giving and receiving, supporting and being supported—these are illusory divisions created by innocent minds trying to make sense of life. How could a mother's care of an infant be any greater a generosity than the infant's expression to the mother as a vulnerable miracle of new life? The gift of a beautiful singer is made whole by the matching gift of an appreciative audience. How can we not be equally grateful for the experience of receiving and the experience of giving?

Terrance was a larger-than-life character in many ways, not always easy, and he made a splash wherever he went. Like a stone tossed into a pond, when Terrance joined the group, we had no idea that his beauty would be revealed and would ripple into the hearts of everyone in the circle. This reciprocity began to reshape the edges of his life, and it filled him with a sense of connection he had been seeking. There is magic in how such beauty is amplified within a circle of hearts that holds experiences collectively. Terrance gradually opened into a newfound peacefulness that marked this new and final year of his life.

Cultivating an Awareness of Mystery

Rather than trying to answer the following questions with your mind, take time to truly inquire into each question separately. If your mind gives you an answer, especially a quick answer, wonder whether it's true. Allow your breath, sound, and the present moment each be living images that answer you through direct experience.

- Where does your next breath come from?

- Where do the sounds that you hear right now come from?

- Where does this present moment come from?

CHAPTER SEVEN

DISCOVERING YOUR
INNER SANCTUARY

*In the midst of winter, I finally learned that
there was in me an invincible summer.*

ALBERT CAMUS

YOU HAVE EMBARKED on a journey, discovered a path to travel inward, and are now ready to enter the abode of your own heart. In the domain of your heart, you will find the source of clarity, wisdom, and compassion that can speak to all your concerns. But where exactly is this doorway of the heart?

Although your heart's door is always open, sometimes our ideas about what it is, where it is, or what it looks like can block our ability to see what is right before our eyes. Our assumptions and expectations can cast an illusionary veil over the heart's entryway.

We inadvertently place blinders over our eyes all the time. Several years ago, I was sitting in a neighborhood diner with a cup of coffee. I was looking all over the tabletop for those little plastic cups of creamer that they always have in diners. When I saw that they had neglected to provide a bowl of them at my table, I signaled the waitress. As I told her my request, she kindly handed me the little silver pitcher filled with cream sitting right in front of me. My eyes were filtering everything on the table through my expectations. Because I knew that cream came in plastic cups, my eyes actually became blind to seeing cream in any other form.

Seeing through the Myths

If you find you are having trouble entering your inner sanctuary, you could be caught in false assumptions about guided imagery. If so, the following exploration of common misconceptions will dismantle these myths and clear the path that welcomes you into your own heart.

■ **Myth #1:** Guided imagery requires a rarified state of consciousness.

In fact, everyone uses imagery all the time. Images are the mind's way of recording and expressing experiences and possibilities. If you have ever worried, dreamed, or fantasized, you have successfully done imagery. But these common forms of imagery are only the tip of the iceberg of what is possible in the internal realms.

If imagery is so natural, you may be wondering why there is so much emphasis on preparing for imagery through traveling inward with breathing exercises, progressive relaxation, and so forth. Related traditions that use imagery such as shamanism or hypnosis even talk about entering a trance state or creating an induction that precedes the images. Aren't these steps referring to entering rarified states of consciousness?

Although a range of internal realms are natural and accessible, most of us are not used to drawing upon many of our inner resources. Our responsibilities as adults are often task-oriented and use the aspects of our minds that plan, analyze, and track accomplishments. Although these capabilities are also natural and valuable, they represent only a very small part of what is available to us. Guided imagery teaches us how to tap into the creative, vital, and nonlinear aspects of consciousness.

Our minds are vast, and although there are a variety of theories about its function and makeup, there is no comprehensive map of consciousness. The more you explore your own inner world, the more you will discover subtle states of awareness and qualities. It's similar to listening to an orchestra. The first time we hear a symphony, the many instruments typically blend into a single auditory experience. But the more we listen, the more we develop discernment of what we hear. We can eventually distinguish the sound of the flute from the clarinet and the oboe. Discernment of consciousness is also cultivated naturally as you spend time exploring your inner terrain.

- **Myth #2:** You have to learn to stop your thoughts before imagery is possible.

Thoughts come and go: there's no stopping them! What we can do, however, is shift our attention so that we are not absorbed in our thinking. The trick is learning how to move our attention.

Consider how the ocean appears choppy with waves. But the deeper we dive below the surface, the more the movement and noise of the water diminishes. So it is with our minds and thoughts. Like the waves, our thoughts continue to come and go, but if our attention is residing in the depths of our minds, there is little impact on our experience from the activity of our thinking.

Take a moment to mentally answer these four questions: What sounds can you hear right now? Where would you like to take a vacation? Do you feel warm, cold, or comfortable? Have you ever been frightened by a dog? Our attention is dynamic and moves so quickly. In less than a minute, these four simple questions prompted our attention to move into the environment and engage our auditory sense, start a fun fantasy, check in with our body, and scan memories for emotional content. And our thoughts continue in this kind of perpetual motion most of the time. What is important is not that there are thoughts, but whether our attention is caught in them.

Most of the time our attention is absorbed in the choppy movement of our thoughts, many of which may not even be true or relevant to the moment. Our thinking tends to repeat itself in well-worn grooves, triggering strong emotions without our even realizing it. As you develop your own familiar pathway to your heart, you may find your attention resides more and more in the spaciousness within.

- **Myth #3:** Guided imagery and visualization are synonymous.

Imagery is not about seeing pictures with the mind's eye. So often I hear, "You know, I tried guided imagery in a workshop, but I just can't visualize any pictures in my mind." Although it's estimated that more than 60 percent of people do have a visual orientation when it comes to internal sense perceptions, there are also kinesthetic impressions, auditory responses, and olfactory memories, all of which are valid portals for the full expression of internal guidance. We often just sense something, and it is accompanied by a feeling that rings true. All of these internal impressions are the language of imagery, and most people have combinations of inner senses that are engaged during the imagery process.

Here is a simple demonstration of just how natural and accessible imagery is. Take a moment to answer this question before you continue: how many doors, including closet doors, do you have in your home?

Unless you recently remodeled, you probably didn't have a number quickly jump to mind. I expect that you took a tour of your home, mentally walked into each room, and looked around. It may not have been a clear, Technicolor movie of your home, but you likely retrieved the information you were after fairly accurately. This is what is important in imagery—having ways to access the information you are after through your internal senses. And it may or may not come through a visual form.

- **Myth #4:** Guided imagery is mind over matter.

Well, sometimes.

This myth speaks to the ongoing debate about the most effective kind of imagery. There are two primary types of imagery, directed and receptive. Directed imagery, which is explored in Chapter 10, asks you to follow a script in order to install a healthy blueprint for physical and emotional well-being. For example, guiding someone with compromised immune responses through a detailed, medically accurate description of a well-functioning immune system would be designed to recalibrate physiology, resulting in more effective and efficient immune responses. This style of imagery can be effective and would be a kind of mind-over-matter approach. But mind over matter is included as a myth because the statement does not represent the full scope of effective imagery approaches.

Although directed imagery can be very useful, it is like going to a clothing store to buy an outfit. You pick something from the rack that looks great, but when you put it on, it may or may not fit. It's hit and miss. Scripted imagery is the same way. The pace may be too fast, too slow, or just right for your process. The images suggested in the script may have meaning for you or they may go against your natural sense of things. Receptive imagery is like going to a tailor who has your exact measurements and knows your style. It is a perfect fit because the source of guidance is you!

Take the example of imagining a relaxing place. What could be better than having someone guide you through a walk on a beautiful beach? The sun is shining, the warm sand is soft under your feet, the fresh breeze caresses your skin, and you hear the sound of the waves. . . .

But stop!

Suddenly your heart—not the sound of waves—is pounding!

If you happen to be someone who nearly drowned at the beach when you were five, the sound of the waves is not soothing. In fact, it triggers a terrifying memory. Your fears are stimulated and the script is having the opposite effect than intended.

Our rich and complex personal histories are embedded within healing symbols. Although some symbols and images seem to share common meanings with a group of people, what is personally healing for any one person at a particular time is very idiosyncratic. Perhaps you have had the experience of picking up a book that you couldn't relate to some years ago, and now it is totally absorbing. There is an organic timing to perspectives that have meaning for us, and receptive imagery takes us right to the source of what is relevant now.

Receptive imagery, the imagery that arises from our hearts, approaches healing from another direction entirely. Using the same example of strengthening the immune system, recall that we saw in Chapter 1 how Roselyn's imagery surfaced from within her own life experience: the birth of kittens from her childhood cat. The images for addressing her immune system were not imposed from the outside but arose from the authority of her innate healing source.

The word *receptivity* comes from the Latin root *re-capere*, meaning "to take back." It suggests reclaiming part of ourselves that may have been covered over, forgotten, or disowned. Receptive imagery retrieves these overlooked parts of us, including the deep well of wisdom within, making them available to us again.

- **Myth #5:** Guided imagery is for relaxing and forgetting about the difficulties of life.

Guided imagery really is an invitation to take your crisis, your worst living nightmare, to the source of tender, compassionate guidance available within your own heart. It is not a process that suggests that you move away from your suffering, but rather promotes embracing the distress so that it can transform.

It is true that relaxation is a part of the preparation for guided imagery, and that imagining a safe and peaceful place is a commonly used and effective stress reduction tool. But this stress management aspect is just a fraction of the rich healing and transformative potential of the guided imagery process.

■ **Myth #6:** You need to believe in the power of imagery in order for it to be effective.

Images have vital impact, regardless of whether we believe them or not. For example, when you are watching an action adventure film, your rational mind knows that the story is fictional and no one is actually in danger of being hurt. But that knowledge doesn't prevent our hearts from racing during a chase scene or keep us from sitting on the edge of our seats during a suspenseful moment. Much of the fun of watching movies is experiencing how our bodies and emotions respond to the images on the screen as though the events were real, even though we know otherwise.

And we respond to the images in our minds in the same way. We believe the images and stories in our heads are real even if they are our fears, projections, or assumptions rather than facts. The habitual, unexamined stories that run through our minds also run our lives. Guided imagery shows you how to bring awareness to these stressful mental images and transform them through the wisdom of your heart.

Identifying Your Inner Sanctuary

With these misconceptions about guided imagery out of your way, you are now ready to discover your inner sanctuary. A sanctuary is a place of refuge, a shelter from danger, a protected area, a sacred place. It is a place where you can be yourself without pressures or expectations. In guided imagery, whether your inner sanctuary is indoors, outdoors, familiar, or new, it's a place where you can be peacefully at home in yourself.

It's likely that you will be surprised at what form your inner sanctuary takes. It is important to notice what image arises rather than predetermining what you think it will be. Greeting the unexpected is a hallmark of imagery. Often I have heard people new to guided imagery anticipating the location they expect to find in advance of the session, only to be amazed at what greets them. Here is what happened for Rachel:

"I had been thinking all week about the upcoming guided imagery session and was anticipating visualizing the really beautiful beach where my husband and I honeymooned in Kauai. After traveling inward through the breathing and relaxation exercises, I invited an image to form for my inner sanctuary and I was amazed to find myself on my grandmother's farm! I haven't been there in maybe thirty years and hadn't thought much about it in the last twenty. But it was perfect. I used to spend the summers there when I was a kid. In the guided imagery, I could see the ripe tomatoes in her prolific vegetable garden and smell the homemade bread. I felt so safe, so held, so . . . okay there, nurtured. I haven't felt so deeply at peace in years."

Your inner sanctuary may be the same each time you travel inward or it may change. Let the image come to you.

The worksheet in Chapter 4 prompts us, "Now that you're relaxed, imagine a place where you can feel even more peaceful." Once the image has appeared, take your time exploring it with as many inner senses as possible. Take in the colors. Experience the textures. Notice the particular sounds, or silence, in your sanctuary. What is the quality of light? What about aromas? What time of day or evening is it? What else do you notice about this amazing place? Find the spot where you can most enjoy your sanctuary, whether sitting, resting, or walking.

Now really notice how you feel being in your inner sanctuary. It is essential that this place is completely safe and comfortable. If there is anything you want or need to make you feel even more empowered and peaceful, invite those changes into your sanctuary. Absorb the qualities of the place. Feel the tranquility above you, below you, before you, behind you, around you, and within you.

But what if your place is not comfortable? What if, in fact, it's rather scary? Or you invite an image for you inner sanctuary, and there are three places that appear? Or there doesn't seem to be a place at all? If you encounter any of these temporary obstacles, here are some specific ways to discover and create your inner sanctuary.

MOVING FROM A SCARY PLACE TO A SAFE PLACE

If you grew up in a chaotic or abusive household, or if you've gone through a traumatic experience that shattered your sense of safety, it may initially be more difficult to enter and sustain a safe place. But what a wonderful gift to give yourself—reestablishing a trustworthy refuge of peace.

If you do not feel completely safe in your sanctuary, here are three ways to promote comfort and ease. You can also blend these approaches to create the place that is just right for you.

- Peel back the layer of threat by imagining that the uncomfortable place that comes to you has an overlay, like a transparent covering, where the dark, uncomfortable images are imprinted. Peel off all the unwanted images and feelings, like they're a decal on a window, eliminating them from the environment. Feel the clear, pristine environment that is restored.

- Ask yourself what you want or need to feel safe, and then invite those elements into your sanctuary. Perhaps your guardian angel keeps watch or a secure fortress surrounds your peaceful place. Maybe an energy dome arcs over you like a powerful force field, or your place is in a secret location that only you can enter. The sky is not the limit; your imagination is.

- If there were a supremely peaceful, safe, beautiful place, what would it be like? Would it be indoors or outdoors? What kind of environment is it, specifically? Describe it in thorough detail. Now step in.

MULTIPLE CHOICE

Invite an image to form for a safe and beautiful place and notice what appears.

"Ah, my garden. How lovely. Wait . . . It's Costa Rica, ummm. Oh! A castle, how splendid!"

Like peering into the window of a bakery, we can become immobilized at the delicious choices available to us. Or with more than one place to choose from, we may get caught in the mental brambles of trying to figure out which place is the right one. There are two simple ways to fully enter one of these sanctuaries.

- Take a moment to really look at and feel each of the images that appear. Does one have more energy than the others? Does one feel more appealing and vibrant? Which one seems to be calling to you right now?

- Take about twenty seconds to step into each of the places, one at a time. Like tasting samples at the bakery, you can directly experience each place and determine which one appeals to you the most right now.

Although each place has something wonderful to offer, the qualities of a place respond to a particular experience that your heart wants you to have right now. Whichever setting comes into focus today, it could very well be one of the other settings in the next imagery journey.

NO PLACE

If you invite an image to form and there is no image, can you be sure this is true? But what, you may ask, if you're sensing . . . nothing?

"Nothing" can be a wonderful place to explore!

What are the characteristics of the nothingness? How big is it? Where is it? Where are the edges of this "nothing"? What color is it? Is it still or does it move?

Healing and Transformation through Self-Guided Imagery

Although this approach may sound silly, or just like a play on words, it is actually a very powerful exploration. Earlier in this chapter we clarified that images are not necessarily visual in nature. So whatever and however you sense nothingness, bring your full awareness to it. Doing so can be a springboard into your inner domain. Trust it and see where it takes you.

Now that you have found a way to abide in a safe and peaceful inner sanctuary, you are ready to go to your Heart of Hearts and receive the generous wisdom that arises from within. You're the One you've been waiting for.

CASE STUDY 7

AMY: FINANCIAL PROBLEMS

The Possible's slow fuse is lit by the imagination.

EMILY DICKINSON

AMY IS A WIDOW in her mid-forties with a son and daughter in high school. She carries complete financial responsibility for managing the household. When her husband died in a car accident several years ago, they had not yet acquired any real assets.

She works full time as an office manager in a busy medical practice and her job is rarely limited to forty hours a week. She is also trying to start up a cosmetics Internet business. She's hoping she can supplement her income this way and eventually generate enough money to free up her time.

They have been getting by, but there are no reserves. It's hand to mouth, month to month, with a fifty-hour workweek because of her two career endeavors. Her kids seem to be doing okay, but she worries that she's too out of the loop with what they are doing and with whom they are spending time. When Amy's not working, she's conscientious about spending time with her kids, as well as just keeping up with laundry, shopping, and all the rest.

114

Amy feels terrible that she has not started a college fund for her kids with high school graduation only a couple years away. She worries about her own retirement. Without owning a home or having investments, her pension plan seems much too meager, and she imagines working as long as it's physically possible for her to do so.

Amy tries her best to be accepting of her situation, and some would describe her as stoic. But beneath the surface, her mind races with worries, a veritable hurricane at times. She feels a constant pressure from not having enough time, enough money, and enough contact with her kids. She usually pops aspirin throughout the day to keep her backache in check, and her dentist has given her a teeth guard to use at night, because there is evidence that she grinds her teeth in her sleep.

Amy yearns for a way out of this constant stress and pressure and is sure the answer lies in just figuring out a way to make more money. There's a part of her that knows she can't maintain this pace forever without an even higher cost to her health. Although she mostly keeps her worries to herself, she has one friend at work whom she confides in. This friend convinced her to try imagery for some stress relief and perhaps a creative look at how she could improve her financial situation.

Journey to the Wisdom of the Heart
SELF-FACILITATION WORKSHEET

1. WHAT DO YOU NEED GUIDANCE ABOUT? (ONE MINUTE)

Write one word or phrase to stand for the topic on which you wish to receive inner guidance from your heart. Make it as short as possible. For example, if your concern is "My ex-husband is late again with a child-support payment. He breaks his agreements time and again. What shall I do?" you would write "my ex" or "finances," depending on which is closest to your real concern.

Write the word or phrase on the piece of paper. Turn the paper over and set it aside, trusting that in just a few minutes, a greater wisdom than you now possess will fully address your concern.

Amy's Topic: *Money*

2. JOURNEY TO YOUR HEART BY TRAVELING INWARD (THREE TO FOUR MINUTES)

The journey to your heart begins as soon as you close your eyes. Bring your attention to your breathing. Each time you breathe in, silently say the word *clarity*. Every time you exhale, silently say the word *peace* and feel your body relaxing. Any time you find your thoughts wandering, bring your focus back to your breath and relaxation. Continue for about three minutes, until you are as relaxed as possible.

Amy's Journey: *As I sit down and follow the instructions for breathing and relaxing, tears just start coming—little sobs. I'm not even sure why. This doesn't feel good, and I consider stopping but decide to go on. I just have to cry for a while. I feel very, very tired all of a sudden. As I breathe out, I feel like black oil is being flushed out of my feet. It's like a car that's overdue for an oil change. I keep crying, but I decide it's okay. It is starting to feel like a release. The oil eventually stops, and I start to feel quiet now. Still exhausted but quiet.*

3. DISCOVERING YOUR INNER SANCTUARY (THREE MINUTES)

Now that you're relaxed, imagine a place where you can feel even more peaceful. It may be a beach, a meadow, or a quiet room in your home. It could even be an imaginary place. Whatever appears, let it be a setting where you can be completely yourself, free from pressures or expectations. Where you find yourself may surprise you, but let your heart show you where it wants to meet you. Even if you have done this process before, you may find yourself in a new environment that is just right for today. Whether you find yourself indoors or outdoors, settle into the most comfortable spot and enjoy the colors, sounds, scents, and feel of this safe and special place.

Amy's Inner Sanctuary: *My inner sanctuary is kind of like a cloud, but more substantial. It's just softness. The essence of softness. It's white but not bright, and everything is quieter here. It's kind of like floating to the bottom of a swimming pool with my eyes closed—the sounds are buffered, and there is weightlessness. There is nothing distinct, no edges or definition. I feel like springs inside me are uncoiling—like a fern opening. It feels very restorative.*

4. BRINGING YOUR TOPIC TO HEART (ONE MINUTE)

Now imagine your paper being delivered to you in this wonderful place. In your mind's eye, view your concern again. Feel your distress embraced by the qualities of your inner sanctuary. Imagine holding your paper and concern lightly in your upturned palms and know that you are about to receive clear guidance from your heart.

Amy's Topic: *Money*

5. RECEIVING YOUR HEART'S MESSAGE (THREE TO FIVE MINUTES)

In your sanctuary, ask your heart for a wise and loving response to your issue. Let your heart's reply appear as an image a few feet in front of you. Whatever symbol appears, receive it as an honored guest. Whether it is a color, a figure, a phrase, or an impression, notice its texture, shape, sound, and so on. Feel the qualities that this image embodies. What does it want you to know about your concern? How do you feel in the presence of your heart's wise advice?

Amy's Heart's Message: *When I focus again on money, it starts to suck me back into pressure and tears. I begin to lose my sanctuary. The money question feels like a giant bowling ball. I go back and forth a few times, back to the cloud, then the ball, and I can eventually remain in my sanctuary with the bowling ball. I ask for my heart's advice. A golden triangle shows up in front of me. It has fumes rising from it. There's no scent; it's visual, the way you can see heat waves rise from asphalt. I think it's a person sitting cross-legged but the features are not very clear and I don't know if it's male or female. The figure asks me to roll the ball over to it. I'll call it "he" but I don't really know. He picks up the bowling ball and tosses it in the air like it's a balloon. I find this deeply insulting, as though he doesn't take my concerns seriously. He's making light of some real problems. He tosses it back to me and asks me hold it in my hands. It's light now, like a beach ball. Then he asks me a series of questions: How will your kids get through college? As I start to answer, the ball gets heavy in my hands. Have you ever been late on your rent? This time, the ball is lighter. He asks me to imagine trying to retire. The weight increases again. Do your kids have everything they need for school this year? Light. We pause, and he tells me that it is not the time or money that is causing my stress, but the way I think about them. He shows me a series of slides from the last several years. It has pictures of our car, home, even a couple of vacations. He tells me that I can have those things with a beach ball or a bowling ball, depending on what game I want to play. And the game takes place in my mind, not in my life. I am completely stunned. I see what he is showing me. He reassures me that it is not about being irresponsible or not taking steps toward a better situation. He's just showing me that if I do it without the heavy thoughts, I will have more energy, happiness, and can even be more productive.*

6. THANKING YOUR HEART (TWO MINUTES)

Thank your heart for the guidance it offered you and allow the image, sound, or impression to fade for now. Know that just as water can be moved from one room to another in a bowl, so too can you carry your heart's wisdom into your daily life in the vessel of your awareness.

Amy's Thanks: *Wow. I'm speechless. Thank you, golden triangle, whatever you are.*

Take a moment in your sanctuary to notice your feelings that linger. Take a moment to let your body, mind, and emotions memorize whatever has been most valuable so that it will be very familiar and accessible to you.

Slowly open your eyes.

You will experience the greatest benefit from this process when your heart's wise advice guides your daily life experience. In the next few minutes, you can integrate the wisdom you have discovered into your life by finding practical steps that transform your insight into action and presence.

DEEPENING YOUR UNDERSTANDING

Take your paper and turn it over with the blank side facing up. Write about or sketch your images and guidance. You may find that additional insights surface at this time. Your writing may simply be words or short phrases, or it may be a continual flow of thoughts and feelings. Don't be concerned about the writing structure. Allow yourself whatever form of expression comes most naturally in the moment.

Amy's Insights: *I draw two circles. One is black and represents the bowling ball. The other I color in with a yellow highlighter, and it is the beach ball. I tape it onto my bathroom mirror so that I can see it in the morning and evening.*

BRINGING YOUR HEART'S WISDOM INTO DAILY LIFE

Is there a specific action you can take to integrate the guidance you just received into your life? Would it involve a conversation with someone or starting a daily practice? Is it about changing or letting go of a pattern? If so, decide specifically where, when, and how you will begin. What is the first step? Write it on your paper with the details of the timeline to which you will commit.

Or perhaps the wise advice from your heart is about a quality, such as patience or courage, that you want to cultivate more fully in your life. What are specific ways that you can stay connected to that quality throughout the day? Can you create touchstones to reconnect yourself to your heart's wisdom, such as putting a symbol on your desk or night-stand or taping a phrase from your writing to your bathroom mirror or dashboard?

Enjoy the wisdom your heart has given you!

Amy's Plan: *I'm really going to do this, and it makes me laugh. I'm stopping by the drugstore after work today and I'm going to buy an inflatable beach ball. I'm going to blow it up and keep it in my bedroom. I look forward to my kids asking me about it. I don't want to teach them to carry worries the way they have seen me. We're doing great. It's time to turn things around for all of us.*

Cultivating an Awareness of Abundance

Do you know how to make God laugh? Tell Him your five-year plan!

I'm sorry, but I have some bad news: There is no way to have security from the world despite our longing for it. Disasters strike even the most sweet, responsible, and conscientious people.

And there is also wonderful news: Look at how you have been taken care of by life. Can you even begin to count the many gifts that have freely come your way? And I include the suffering we have all had in the count. Life is rich, and all experiences are part of a remarkable, sacred journey of being human.

We are completely dependent on whatever this force is that animates life. What if we align our lives with this powerful and creative force rather than relying on our cleverness to shape our lives? What an adventure. Are you ready to risk everything to have everything?

Are you living in the place now that you pictured you would be five years ago? Are you doing what you thought you would be doing? How about one year ago? Accurate predictions are random and short-lived and most enjoyable as a headline in the tabloids.

Life will take you where it does, with and without your thought about how it should go. Can you feel what it would be like to align with life's intelligent flow with your full being, saying "yes" to the richness of your one and only life?

- Right now, just in the very moment, not minutes ahead or behind, let life as you are experiencing it be a living image. What is it expressing to you?

- Think of something you dislike doing around the house—the dishes . . . taking out the trash . . . folding clothes. Notice the thoughts that accompany the chore: "I have better things to do . . . It's boring. . . . It's a waste of time."

Now try an experiment. Do the task without the resistance, without the mental commentary. If you wash the dishes, notice the feeling of the warm soapy water on your hands, the lemony smell of the soap, the way the light glistens on the smooth, wet surface of a plate. How delicious.

Notice how it is the same basic life experience whether we push it away or enjoy it. The difference is whether your attention is absorbed in negative thinking or whether you experience life directly in the moment without the mental commentary. How is life here for you, right now?

- Start a gratitude list. Jot down a few of the things you're grateful for right now. You may want to included the surprise packages: seeing the flower that was growing between the cracks of the cement; going one more day without smoking a cigarette; a zero percent credit card offer in the mail (perfect timing); a rich conversation with a close friend who shared the ways that I'm insensitive (how valuable!); the aspirin that relieved my headache; enjoying the sunlight on my shoulders during my coffee break. Feel the gratitude. Let the feeling be a living image. Give the feeling a voice. What is being expressed?

Healing and Transformation through Self-Guided Imagery

CHAPTER EIGHT

RECEIVING YOUR HEART'S GUIDANCE

And now here is my secret, a very simple secret;
it is only with the heart that one can see rightly,
what is essential is invisible to the eye.

ANTOINE DE SAINT-EXUPÉRY

THERE IS A BUDDHIST STORY in which a teacher and student meet by a mountain lake for spiritual instruction. The student is asked to put a heaping tablespoon of salt into a glass of water, stir it, and then taste it. Following the directions, the student quickly spits out the water, complaining of the bitter taste. The teacher then asks that the student stir the same amount of salt into the lake and drink the lake water. When the student tastes the water, it is sweet to his tongue.

"Your troubles are like the salt," comments the teacher.

"It is the same amount of suffering whether they are contained in a limited perspective, like the glass, or if you surround them with spaciousness, like the lake. The difference is that in your small-mindedness, you experience them as bitter, and in your spaciousness, they are sweet."

Bringing your topic of concern into your inner sanctuary is bringing the salt of your suffering into spaciousness. The jagged edges of stress that are so painful when they circulate in the narrow tracks of the

123

mind can now be surrounded by the open, loving compassion of your heart's sanctuary.

Revisiting Your Topic

Although most of the time it is easy to bring a stressful issue into an inner sanctuary, there are three common obstacles that occasionally arise. For each of these themes, there is a simple solution.

Are you settling for bliss rather than transformation? Discovering your inner sanctuary can be such a profoundly peaceful experience, especially after a prolonged period of stress, that it is tempting to remain in a blissful state without revisiting the original concern. Although absorbing the peaceful qualities in the environment can be a valuable experience in and of itself, to stop at this point prevents transformation at the source of the crisis. The result is that the relief will only be temporary. Ease and calmness will be accessible in your inner sanctuary, but when you are back in the flow of your life, it's likely that the painful feelings will arise again. By continuing with the imagery journey, the entire process can shift your perspective in a substantial way that uproots the source of the painful feelings and allows peace to become part of your daily life.

Are you reidentifying with the concern? When we are in a crisis state, most of us revisit painful memories time and again: at 3:00 in the morning; daydreaming in the middle of a meeting; describing them to a friend over coffee. Recent research in neuropsychology tells us that these mental habits of revisiting past events actually create neural pathways in the brain, reinforcing the painful memory. It is like carving a path in a forest that becomes more clearly defined with regular use. Our attention then responds like a trained horse that automatically follows the familiar path and returns home to the pain. If this happens during the imagery journey, we can lose the experience of our sanctuary and become reabsorbed in the distress.

When you imagine revisiting your topic, continue to feel the qualities of your sanctuary around you, and hold your concern lightly. Consider what it takes to hold water in your hands. There needs to be enough firmness to form a cup with your palms. But if you grab the water or if your hands are too slack, the water will slip through your fingers. You want to find the middle ground when focusing on your concern. Hold it gently in your awareness without grasping but with enough attention to revisit the issue.

Try cupping your hands in front of your heart while you are in your sanctuary, letting the paper with your word or phrase on it rest lightly in your upturned palms.

If you do get drawn back into your pain, simply open your eyes and begin again with breathwork or another relaxing approach to traveling inward. You may also benefit from taking more time in your sanctuary before revisiting your topic. As with all aspects of the imagery journey, your abilities to maintain inner focus will grow with practice.

Are you afraid of contaminating your sanctuary? In Chapter 7 we explored how beauty, safety, and tranquility are the natural characteristics of an inner sanctuary. To introduce a frightening, violent, or despairing life experience into that setting can sound like pouring pollutants into a pristine stream. But bringing the most shameful experiences, harshest judgments, and rawest wounds into your own heart is how healing happens. It is the pain that changes, not your sanctuary.

It is possible to bring your greatest living nightmare into your inner sanctuary without contamination because within you is the source of life that is indestructible and incorruptible. This is the very nature of the wellspring within your own heart. There is no terror so large, no pain so deep, no suffering so perpetual, that it could harm your heart's natural wholeness.

There is an important distinction between your life and your life conditions. Your life is the enduring miraculous force that animates you and all things, the strange and beautiful mystery of how, why, and what you are. We encounter infinitely pure life in the domain of our heart. Your life conditions, on the other hand, are the circumstances that shift and change: relationships, dwellings, achievements, possessions, points of view, and age, to name a few. Our suffering arises from our attitudes toward the shifts in our life conditions—the loss of a relationship, the death of a dream. Pains arising from the changes in these life conditions are what become identified for a guided imagery journey and brought to our hearts for healing.

Although losses can be completely overwhelming, when you bring your suffering into the vastness of your heart with guided imagery, the perspective shifts. Like the salt that dissolves in the vastness of the lake, your suffering transforms through the magnitude of your heart's wisdom.

Discover the you that is even more vast and deep than a lake. Ask yourself the question, Who is it that is aware of thoughts, feelings, and sensations?

If it is hard to trust that compassion and peace are stronger than your pain, try this experiment. In your imagery journey, act as though it were true that you could trust a source of wisdom greater than you know. Find out what happens.

RECEIVING YOUR HEART'S MESSAGE

There is a Greek proverb that says, "Wonder is the beginning of wisdom." Wonder is our natural state of being when we are experiencing the miracle of life without the filters of mental beliefs. And it feels wonder-*ful* to be full of wonder. The state of open curiosity, wonder, is the key to receiving our heart's message.

The natural process of guided imagery usually flows easily. We most often get into trouble when we interfere with the process by interjecting our thoughts, trying too hard, and dismissing what appears in imagery. Here are a few common ways that we get in our own way at this point in the journey.

Are you rejecting what appears? In Chapter 5, we read about Stan's cave imagery. His heart had profound insights for his life, but because the form of his heart's voice was so unexpected, he almost dismissed it. Luckily, Stan didn't follow the voice in his head that said, "My heart is speaking to me as a crab?! Don't hearts speak as wise figures or rays of light or something?"

Images can arise in any form, and they are typically unexpected although consistently relevant. The whole point is to move beyond the same old perspectives. And given that the images arise from beyond our conscious awareness, it's not surprising that they are surprising!

Another client I worked with had a guided imagery session where there was a lively conversation between an angel and a devil. Her eyes kept popping open during the session, and with an amazed look on her face, she'd comment, "I don't believe in these things!" Then she'd close her eyes and continue. She suspended her logical objections in order to yield to the wisdom that the images imparted. She was glad she did. Although her wisdom took a puzzling form, she was able to get the guidance she needed from these unexpected images.

Try approaching everything you experience during the imagery journey as perfect, just the way it appears. Whatever image comes forth, whether it makes sense to you or not, take time to explore the colors, textures, and qualities. Take the image in as though you were greeting a welcome guest.

Are you projecting what you expect? Remember that this form of imagery is a receptive process. While other imagery approaches ask that you intentionally create specific symbols, this imagery journey invites you to allow an image to form and notice what appears. Because many of us are so skilled at making things happen through effort, we sometimes slip into this same active approach when receptivity is needed. It is counter-productive in this process to will an image into focus.

To anticipate your heart's answer is like being in a conversation with a friend and not letting her speak because you "know" what she is going to say. Your prediction may or may not be true, but you definitely close the door to finding out.

Turn your palms upward. Listen. Keep it simple. Let go. Notice. Watch. Take your time. Allow.

Are you greeting a wolf in sheep's clothing? Sometimes a response appears in our inner sanctuary that can seem like the voice of our heart when it's not. So what is that other voice, and how do we discern our heart's message?

We all have many inner parts, or "selves"—the critic, the child, the stoic, the clown, to name just a few. Many of these parts are fun and even helpful in certain life situations. However, when we have a deeply ingrained habit of acting from one of these selves in daily life, it may rise up automatically, disguised as the voice of your heart.

Let's say that you have a strong inner critic and you bring a possibility of launching a new career into your sanctuary for exploration. If your critic comes forth, the answer you receive may be a familiar rant of old judgments: "Forget it. You don't have what it takes. You'd be a fool to try."

Whether it turns out to be the right time for a career change or not, the voice of the critic blocks the opportunity to explore a fresh perspective from your wise heart.

There are ways to cultivate discernment for spotting a wolf in sheep's clothing. Test the voice that appears with these three criteria:

- Inquire. Is the voice or symbol that appears truly wise, trustworthy, loving, and compassionate? Is it knowledgeable about you and the topic you are bringing forth? Ask the symbol directly.

- Use your "felt sense." Eugene Gendlin, in his book *Focusing*, the term *felt sense* is a description of our body's innate intelligence. Pay attention to how the voice or symbol in your inner sanctuary feels in your body. Does the message ring true with your experience of a loving, compassionate response?

- Remember that your heart's wise advice is typically surprising. Does the information feel like the same familiar point of view that you have already mulled over, or does it have a fresh, unexpected perspective?

If you discover that an inner self is masquerading as your heart in your inner sanctuary, simply thank it for coming and dismiss it. Then begin again by inviting the loving voice of your heart to appear.

Are you getting lost in the land of the "what ifs"? Receptive imagery has us face directly into the unknown, and this can be very disconcerting, especially if the issues being explored concern our health status or a relationship we don't want to lose or job difficulties that might throw us into financial chaos. *What if* we don't like the answer we receive from our heart? Or *what if* nothing appears? *What if* there are three answers? Our internal "what if" generator is very creative, and it can spew out lists of reasons not to proceed. It is fueled by fear. We wouldn't be doing this guided imagery process if at least some part of us didn't want to explore and resolve the issue. But sometimes our fear-based parts surface and whisper in our ears, "Are you sure you really want to know?"

The truth is that we are all experts at facing directly into the unknown. When have we ever seen beyond this moment? Do you really know what will occur in five minutes, in one minute?

Many of our plans and expectations come to pass, but many do not. We get in the habit of believing we can see beyond this moment, but it doesn't take much investigation to realize that we have always been blinded to what the future will truly bring.

Trust your expertise to be with whatever arises. You have been doing this successfully your whole life. Where's the proof? Here you are!

Know that whatever you hear from your heart is not an order to do something. It is just an opportunity to receive new information. You can still use all your considerations and resources to take action, or not.

Thanking Your Heart

Discovering your inner sanctuary and receiving your heart's wisdom is like developing a new relationship, and it is a new, loving relationship with yourself. If you enjoyed a wonderful meal with a friend, or received expert advice from a consultant, or felt the compassionate presence of a teacher, it would be natural to express thanks at the end of your time together. And your heart does provide nourishment, guidance, and presence. To thank your heart for meeting you in this way is to invite even more intimate, ongoing rendezvous.

There is a great range of benefits to expressing gratitude for your heart's participation. Robert Emmons at UC Davis and Michael McCullough at the University of Miami published research in the *Journal of Personality and Social Psychology* on the psychological and physical impact of gratitude. In the experiment, participants were asked to keep track of their experiences of gratitude. A few of the benefits they reported include greater progress toward important personal goals; higher levels of alertness, enthusiasm, determination, and energy; and a greater sense of connection to others.

There is also a mysterious, natural connection between the heart and gratitude. Take a moment to remember someone you really love, to whom you feel grateful. Notice the feelings that are present in your chest. There is often a sensation of swelling or expanding. Many poems and ballads describe this phenomenon: a heart on fire, a heart soaring with wings, a heart as big as the ocean. The reason that these kinds of images are so prevalent is that they are so relatable. Gratitude lets us dip into the deep well of love in our hearts.

As you express gratitude, note anything specific that seems valuable, interesting, or curious that has come from your imagery journey. Imprint these new feelings onto your body, mind, and emotions. Let the new sensations become familiar so that they remain very accessible to you, and easy to return to.

A Seamless Transition

The transition from the inward focus of imagery to opening your eyes again is a vital and often overlooked step of the process. You are not leaving your imagery experience behind as you open you eyes. Rather, when you open your eyes, you are bringing your new feelings and fresh perspectives into your life.

It is easy for old thought habits to be triggered when our senses become bombarded again with input from the world. Because we have so many associations with the objects in our environment—where and when we acquired the living room table, what we were doing when we wore that dress—we can quickly get absorbed in habitual thoughts and behaviors when we reenter our physical world. It is really worth developing a slow and mindful transition to maintain the greatest benefits from the guided imagery work.

Try opening your eyes for just ten seconds or so and then closing them again to sustain your fresh imagery perspectives. Continue alternating with open and closed eyes, gradually expanding the duration you are able to have your eyes open while experiencing your new feelings and perspectives.

So the challenge now is clear: to take the wisdom from our hearts and let it guide us in moment-to-moment living. We can integrate our imagery journey in a way that frees us from the habitual cycle of distressing thoughts and feelings. And there are a number of tools to do just that.

Healing and Transformation through Self-Guided Imagery

KAREN: MARITAL ISSUES—ANGER

*Holding onto anger is like grasping a hot coal
with the intent of throwing it at someone else;
you are the one who gets burned.*

GAUTAMA BUDDHA

"I'M AT A COMPLETE LOSS. I've tried everything." Karen reaches for the Kleenex, her face creasing from restrained tears. "Tim and I get into these fights. He gets so angry! We lock horns and can't seem to resolve anything. It's horrible. It's a cycle, and each time it happens I feel even more disheartened. There's lots of love in our marriage, two great kids, some really fun times, but I'm afraid these conflicts are eroding our relationship. There are times I wonder whether we should stay together." This confession brings on another eruption of tears.

Karen goes on to describe the ways their fights linger in her body for several days: tightness in her stomach that affects her appetite, digestion, and sleep. She finds herself walking on eggshells in the hope of not triggering another argument. "I get angry that he gets so angry but I know it's not all his fault. I wonder what's wrong with me." Her body crumples into the chair. "I just don't know what to do. It's been going on a long time, and nothing we've tried has helped."

Karen and I have worked together off and on for a number of years, and she's comfortable and familiar with the guided imagery process. She's willing to see what insights imagery could yield by exploring this painful dilemma. We begin.

"Find a comfortable position to relax in the chair. Let your breath find it's way into an even flow. Feel the natural rise and fall of the breath and make room for it in your belly. Breathe in, inviting the qualities of calm and ease. Breathe out, noticing the natural releasing qualities of the exhalation." We spend time dissolving the tightness in her stomach that formed in the recounting of the stressful memories. Gradually, there is softness to her face, and I see her body subtly give way into the cushions of the chair. "Invite an image to appear for a safe place for today's exploration."

"I'm on a stage. It's an elegant theater. It's old, beautiful. There's a gold curtain and dark wood. The lights on stage are bright—dazzling. I twirl onto the stage from the wings, wearing a tutu—like in *Swan Lake*. In the light, it's iridescent, pearly, and shimmering. I'm extending through my arms first to the right and then to the left, acknowledging the space around me. I can feel the light on my face. I'm graceful and poised: it's exhilarating! I used to dance quite often in my youth. I loved it. The feeling of gracefulness is familiar and natural. I'm so glad to experience this again."

I encourage her to really notice how the experience of gracefulness, being full of grace, is present in her body, mind, and emotions. "Let this way of being with yourself become very accessible. Let those qualities amplify and take time to be in grace right now." We pause, letting the silence deepen the experience.

"Is this a good time and place to explore the anger issue in your marriage?" I inquire. She says yes, and invites an image to arise related to her husband. Tim appears in the wings with a pinched, angry look on his face, leaning forward on his feet. He's in his familiar beige shorts and worn green T-shirt. As if in slow motion, he lobs a glowing red globe toward her. She recognizes this ball as anger. "I see it coming toward me, and as I do the most beautiful curtsey, it passes right over me."

Karen has always been triggered by Tim's anger, escalating the conflict. But this image is offering her a new possibility.

"What's that like for you?" I ask.

"It's so simple," she responds quietly.

We pause again in the silence as this awareness takes hold in her. She's surprised by the ease of the solution that has been an obstacle for so long.

"This is amazing. I don't have to take on his anger. I see I can stay true to myself when he's angry. I can bow to him; acknowledge just how he is in this moment. When I do this, I even feel warmth toward him because I see how he's frustrated and I know that's not what he really wants either."

As Karen rests in the aftermath of these images with her eyes closed, her face looks completely different—more youthful and relaxed.

When the session feels complete, I guide her attention back to the room and inquire what impressed her the most about the imagery experience. "The love. I never expected that the most painful and distressing times with Tim could shift into a loving feeling so easily. I feel a genuine love flowing out toward him from my heart. And I feel so much more loving toward myself, too."

Anger can be a vital expression to protect healthy personal boundaries, a passion against injustice, a driving force to create change. And yet when it becomes a habitual response or hardens into the feature of a personality, it can quickly escalate, becoming a destructive force toward oneself and relationships. Through the imagery, Karen found a way to free herself from the anger pattern that has volleyed between the two of them for years. She discovered an opening to her own grace and graciousness, regardless of the mood or behavior of her husband. The bow became an outer expression of an inner surrender, and that gentle but powerful gesture broke an old pattern. The surprising result was love flowing naturally.

It only takes one person to create a radical transformation within a relationship. Like a mobile sculpture, the entire balance of a relationship is reconfigured when one of the elements shifts. With Karen's new approach, this doesn't necessarily mean that Tim will change. But as he's met in a different way, without the familiar pushback from Karen, that experience alone will open new possibilities for him.

"How do we 'ground' the inspiration from the imagery into practical action? What does it mean to bow in actual interactions with her husband?" These questions become the subject that Karen and I explore over the next several weeks.

As a first step, she decides to tell Tim about her imagery, and she relates her experience in our next session.

"At first he was defensive. He was making fun of me as a dancer. But when I was telling him how much I love him, he relaxed, and we had a really nice connection. I let him know that I'm going to literally bow, at least my head, at times when we get into our old patterns and I have enough presence of mind to remember. It's really a practice for me, but I'm hoping it can be a reminder for him too of the kind of relationship we both want and can have. He seems to really appreciate this."

It's not surprising that in the weeks that followed, Karen reported her success as patchy. "Three steps forward, two steps back," I reminded her, "is a common rhythm of change." We did another imagery session to see whether there was more that could support her new practice, and a surprising new dimension surfaced.

With a brief induction, she dropped deeply into an imagery state:

"I'm in a field. No—I don't know where I am. It's so beautiful. Bright. Golden. I don't know where my body stops and the air begins. Things look delicate, transparent, fragile, and yet the feeling is of tremendous . . . um, strength, vitality. There's no *me*, but I'm everywhere, like drops of moisture glistening in the air. If I wiggle my invisible toes, I see only wheat grasses rippling across the field. I recognize the breeze as my breath. My heartbeat hums through distant crickets. I am immense, immeasurable, and yet the tiniest pebble sends waves of joy through me. It's peace. It's vitality. It's life."

This imagery session was pivotal for Karen and marked a deep reorientation in her life as a whole. Although we started out focusing on her marriage, as her energy was largely freed from that concern in her life, it opened up new vistas. This natural deepening is prevalent with the guided imagery process. Although the relationship continued to be a theme in our ongoing work together, it was becoming secondary to her desire to cultivate an ongoing experience of the interconnectedness of life. "I want to be able to feel that core of peace within me, no matter what the state of my marriage, no matter what is happening in my life. I've read about this for a long time and now I have a taste. I know it's possible."

Learning to let go of a painful dynamic within her marriage became the natural preparation for surrendering to life on a larger scale. Karen was learning to bow with grace to all that life presents.

EYES OPEN IMAGERY:
Cultivating an Awareness of Surrender and Connection

Like Karen, is there a recurring pattern in your life that binds your energy and causes you distress? What would it be like to bow to this person or situation? This doesn't mean putting up with bad behavior or neglecting to set healthy boundaries. Choose a situation where acceptance is the healthy response:

- Pick a specific situation where you can practice bowing with grace. It can be performed as an internal movement visible only to your own heart. Notice how surrendering connects you to your own open heart and makes more room for loving yourself and others.

- Look at a familiar object in your home—perhaps something like a plain, wooden chair. That chair could not be yours without the breath, hands, and hearts of thousands and thousands of people.

Consider just the nails that hold the chair together. There are the miners who extracted the raw metal from the earth, the team that designed the size and type of nail, the manufacturers who shaped the nails on precise machinery, and the mechanics who kept the machines functioning. Then there are the people who designed and produced the containers the nails came in, along with the deli workers who made lunch for them. Imagine the office of the sales and marketing team and the artist who designed the packaging labels. The nails arrived at the warehouse and store by truck on roads built and maintained by engineers and construction crews, and so on. This is only a fraction of the people on the nail committee. We could outline the same kind of interconnected contributions with the wood, stain, glue, and so on.

Let the chair be a living image of the thousands of hands and hearts that enter your life in essential and unseen ways every day. What is your chair, a living image, expressing to you?

- What are the ways that your presence connects you to others? There are obvious answers based on your friendships and professional activities, but let's explore the subtle and powerful ways we are impacting each other all the time.

Have you ever observed a loving couple affectionately walking down the street and transferred that sweet atmosphere to your own partner through a hug and kiss? Have you taken to heart something an acquaintance shared with you years ago, perhaps someone you are no longer in touch with but still value for her guidance to this day? Have you ever overheard a conversation at a neighboring table in a café, learning from it as if you were part of that circle of friends?

Know that you too have been observed! You can't possibly know the extent of the value and meaning of what may have occurred when you smiled at a stranger in the doctor's waiting room or joked with a cashier or held open the door for someone with an armload of packages.

We are giving and receiving all the time. Everything is expressive and receptive, and connection is always flowing. Let the next person you see be a living image of what life is so generously here to share with you right now.

CHAPTER NINE

INTEGRATING WISDOM INTO ACTION AND PRESENCE

Be the change you want to see in the world.

MOHANDAS GANDHI

HAVE YOU EVER arrived home from a vacation with the thought, "I'm going to make this relaxing feeling last," but in just a day or two, you're wrapped up in the old pace and pressure of daily life? Or perhaps you experienced a particularly insightful guided imagery journey and thirty minutes later you're tense and frustrated in the car when road-work created an unexpected traffic jam. How is it that calm states can feel so stable and lasting in one moment but can then shift so quickly in the next?

Researchers at MIT have confirmed one answer to this question that we have known instinctually for quite some time: we are all creatures of habit. In *New Scientist* magazine, Mark Buchanan describes how Alex Pentland, head of MIT's Media Lab, studied just how much of the time we are acting out of habit in our daily life. He monitored people by strapping electronic devices onto them that record a range of information, such as tone of voice, pace and location of travel, and subtle body language. The subjects then went about their lives—working, sleeping, eating, and enjoying leisure activities. Although we love to think of ourselves as conscious beings with free will, the results of the research revealed that close to 90 percent of what most people do in any given day follows routines that are directed by unconscious instincts.

So when we get into our car, however deep the imagery journey may have been just moments before, a distinct array of habits and instincts kick in, summoned by the familiarity of driving. Our habits take root in our thoughts, emotions, and physical instincts. For example, drivers who typically rush to work will habitually gear up for speed whether or not they are actually short on time. So the act of driving puts us on automatic pilot, rather than setting us up to respond to the immediate situation. And the driving habit supercedes the experience of the relaxation.

Another clue that explains why we can have radical, swift changes in awareness is found in what is known as *state-dependent learning*. The basic premise is that we can best recall something we have learned when we are in the same state of mind as when we first learned it. In other words, memory is state dependent—if we are in a low mood, it is much more likely that we will recall sad events rather than happy ones. If we are in a relaxed state with an open, calm mind, the insights gleaned from imagery will be much more readily accessible.

The good news is that there are a variety of ways to bring our heart's wisdom from guided imagery into the fluctuations of day-to-day life. We can stop reacting to our habitual triggers of stress and let wisdom become the natural guide to our thoughts, feelings, and actions. And as we integrate the insights from imagery into moment-to-moment living, our lives transform. Let's explore some specific ways to integrate wisdom into actions and presence.

Deepening Your Understanding

You may have noticed that if you tell someone a dream soon after awakening from sleep, the meaning of the dream often becomes clearer through telling the story. When we take an internal experience and express it outwardly, the process helps us connect the dots, deepening our understanding. Using words activates a different part of our brain from the area where images are seen and felt. By verbalizing the images, we are expanding and linking together several ways of knowing.

Describing a dream to someone also makes it much easier to recall the dream later. It's as though telling the dream makes it even more real. And this is literally true. The dream, which had only been our inner impressions, now has taken the tangible outer form of words. And two people know the dream now, instead of only one. The process of creating, of manifesting ethereal impressions into material forms, is alchemy; it's magic. And it happens all the time.

Take a look at your home for a moment. There was a point in time when it didn't exist. Then there was a point when it was only an idea in someone's mind. There was a time when it was just a drawing. At some point, the image of a building was described to others. And, through many other steps, the place is now a very real part of your life. First there was nothing; now there is something. The invisible became real, tangible, and useful. You could say that the building was born out of an image.

The same process applies with your imagery journeys as well. We can start to weave imagery experiences into daily life by first expressing the images in writing, drawing, or movement. By translating the subtle inner experience of imagery into words, colors, shapes, and sensations, they begin to take on more concrete forms. Just as with the creation of a building, the images of your heart's wisdom can also start to gain substance when they belong not only to your inner world, but become part of the outer physical world as well.

The benefits of expressing our images are twofold: As our inner images take an outward form, they become more real in day-to-day moments. And as we can see, touch, and read about our experiences, the process stimulates new insights, adding to the richness of our inner perspectives. Our inner and outer worlds enrich each other if we consciously bridge these domains. As the Sufi saying goes, we "materialize the spiritual and spiritualize the material."

So how can you deepen your understanding of your imagery journey? Write it and draw it! You may find that one mode works better for you than another, and it would be valuable to give each one a try. You can also blend them together, for example, by sketching an image and then writing about it.

JOURNALING

Whenever possible, take time to write down your inner experiences immediately after you open your eyes at the end of an imagery journey. Keep it simple. Start with a description of your inner sanctuary and the image and message of your heart's guidance. Then break free of sequential thinking. Just note any other impressions, feelings, and images that arise as you write.

The purpose of this kind of writing is not to create publishable prose or poetry. The words don't even need to fit together into full sentences, and the writing doesn't need to make sense to anyone else. We learn in Dore Ashton's editing of Picasso's works in *Picasso on Art* that the artist scribbled this revealing note in the back of one of his sketchbooks: "Painting is stronger than me, it makes me do its bidding." In a similar way, let the writing take hold of you. Send your inner critic on a vacation and just let words flow.

Here are a few tips to get you started:

- Write without stopping. So much of what we have covered about relaxation and imagery emphasizes pausing and stillness. With this exercise, the opposite is true. The reason is that although we are engaging the mind by using language, we still want creative expression without interpretations. Sustaining the flow of writing helps keep the analytical mind in check.

- Don't use a pretty journal. You want to stay involved in the process of writing rather than focusing on the final product. In other words, if you are trying to make a lovely book, that goal could limit the impulses that you may want to give expression to. Maybe it will feel right one day to rip a page or scribble. That might feel perfect, but if it clashes with the goal of a particular aesthetic, it would dampen the creative flow.

- Write a minimum of three pages. Three pages can seem like a vast sea of paper when it rests empty before you. Often it's when you write beyond what you can think of to say that the most valuable and juicy insights come forth.

- Protect your privacy. If there is a risk that someone else may read what you are writing, it is likely that your inner editor will interrupt the free expression of your innermost feelings. If you are writing longhand, find a safe place to store your journal. If you prefer to write on a computer, find a web page that is password protected.

Having a journal can also be a fast track back to your wise self. If you're upset and don't have the time for a full imagery session, reading a journal entry can reconnect you with wisdom that you have already discovered.

DRAWING AND COLLAGE

It can be very freeing to let your images and feelings express themselves in colors and designs rather than words. Georgia O'Keeffe says it beauti-

Healing and Transformation through Self-Guided Imagery

fully in the Hunter Drohojowska-Philip bibliography, *In Full Bloom: The Art and Life of Georgia O'Keeffe*. "I found I could say things with color and shapes that I couldn't say any other way—things I had no words for." Just as with journaling, the aim is not to create a "product" (in this case, a picture ready for framing), but to use drawing as an outlet to further explore your imagery. If you are feeling tranquil, perhaps you will smear a smooth blue arc on a sheet of paper. Or if you are working through distress, maybe you will draw jagged black spikes.

So even if you are one of those people who claim, "I can't draw," this way of exploring is still open to you. The natural drawing that we all felt free to do as children is all that's needed. Your drawing does not have to be a reproduction of the images. Perhaps the colors and shapes are suggestive of the mood of your experience.

Here are a few tips to get you started. These exercises are all designed to move past the tendency to veto this form of exploration. Start your drawing just as soon as you complete your imagery journey:

- Draw with your eyes closed. Let your hand move with the feeling of the image without checking the paper. Stay with it until you feel it's complete. When you open your eyes, you may be inclined to judge how accurately this drawing compares to what you expected to see. Instead, try looking at the paper as though it is exactly what you intended. Look at it as though someone else created it. What do you see?

- Draw with your nondominant hand. If you are right-handed, draw with your left hand. Our dominant side tends to be more ingrained with habits and control. Let yourself draw, happily out of control.

- Draw without lifting your pen from the paper. This is another approach that helps us break the expectations of how drawings "should" be. It's wonderful what is created when we draw outside the lines.

There is no need to invest in expensive art materials, but it would be helpful to get some kind of drawing materials with a range of colors. I suggest oil pastels or colored pencils that have a soft, thick lead. There are also inexpensive felt-tip markers available now, which range from bold to pastel colors. All of these mediums work well on almost any kind of paper.

Collage is also a very easy way to work with colors and shapes. While still in the mode of your imagery experience, flip through a magazine and cut out pictures and phrases that appeal to you. Just as with the guided imagery, you don't need to know why a particular image draws your attention or what it means. Trust your intuition.

The images may be from ads or articles—it doesn't matter. When possible, have a variety of types of magazines: *Sports Illustrated, Scientific American, Gourmet*—the more, the merrier. If you don't have access to magazines, see whether your doctor's office will give you the old editions from the waiting room as they are replaced with newer magazines. Cut and arrange the pictures and phrases on a poster board or large sheet of paper, securing them with a glue stick. When the collage feels complete, give it a title. If possible, have the collage out for at least a week in a place where you can see it often. Pay attention to what else you may notice about it during the week. Let it continue to be a living image that speaks to you.

Bringing Your Heart's Wisdom into Daily Life

In Tibet, many of the public plazas have prayer wheels. These wheels are cylinders inscribed with prayers that are attached to a spindle. As someone passes by, the wheel is spun when brushed with the palm of a hand,

and this action is believed to release prayers and induce a meditative mind. The spinning of the wheel reminds the person of his deeper self.

Prayer wheels are a type of touchstone, an active symbol of remembrance. We can create any number of touchstones for tapping into our imagery experience anytime, anywhere. The first type we will explore is called an anchor.

ANCHORS

Anchoring is a natural process that usually occurs without our awareness. For example, a favorite love song can be an anchor to romantic feelings. Viewing a photograph of a treasured vacation spot is an anchor that will reawaken a relaxed mood. The smell of cinnamon toast can anchor our feelings to warm childhood memories. Developed by Bandler and Grinder in an approach called neurolinguistic programming (NLP), an *anchor* is a link, or an association, between a state of being and something else, often a person, a place, an object, or a sensation.

We can also intentionally create anchors to states of being that we want to cultivate in our life. Here's how to anchor the open, relaxed qualities of a guided imagery journey into daily life.

When you are doing a guided imagery session and are in your inner sanctuary, press together the thumb and pointer finger of your nondominant hand (if you are right-handed, then use your left hand), exerting just enough force so that you can feel a mild sensation of pressure. At the same time, keep the image and feeling of your sanctuary and silently say one word that describes a quality you are experiencing. It could be a word such as "calm," "free," or "loved." By doing this, you are anchoring your state of being to the sensation in your hand, an image, and a word. Hold your anchoring hand gesture for about thirty seconds before continuing with your imagery session.

You can now use this anchor anytime, anywhere. When you have a moment during the day, maybe a coffee break at work, take a few minutes to close your eyes and use your anchor, pressing together your thumb and finger, while silently repeating the word that describes the quality of your inner sanctuary and recalling the image of the environment. Notice the state of being that is evoked. Try using your anchor initially in a fairly quiet moment. You can eventually call upon this fast track to peace even in the most stressful times.

You can anchor not only to your inner sanctuary but also to the guidance you receive from you heart during your imagery journey. To do this, design a new anchor specific to the insight, using a different combination of a movement, a sensation, an image, and a word. For example, the movement could be bowing your head or pressing the tip of your tongue to the roof of your mouth or squeezing an earlobe. It can be anything, as long as it feels right to you. Again, blend a sensation with a word representing a quality, along with the image. Let it be simple, clear, and consistent.

RITUAL

Ritual is another form of anchoring but in an even more active form. A ritual can be any sequence of actions, usually repeated in the same way each time, coupled with an intention to create and reproduce a desired state of being. Common examples would be lighting candles or incense while saying a prayer, but it could just as effectively include putting on your shoes with gratitude if the action is performed with the same quality of attentiveness.

Betty created a ritual that came out of her guided imagery session. She was struggling with intense grief over the sudden death of her husband Jim. They had been married for forty-one years, and the loss sent her into a tailspin, where she lost her appetite, spent much of her day in tears, and had difficulty sleeping. She began to experience chest pain that her doctor attributed to high levels of anxiety.

Healing and Transformation through Self-Guided Imagery

When Betty traveled to her inner sanctuary, she asked for an image of her grief to appear. It was her heart charred like the smoldering ash that trails a wildfire. She continued and asked for guidance, and the response was deeply moving.

The image was Jim's hands pouring clear, cool water from a pitcher into her heart. As he filled her heart with soothing relief, he spoke the words, "We can be connected in peace, my beloved. I want this for you."

This experience had a strong impact on Betty. To keep the image with her, she created a ritual where every morning she fills a crystal bowl with water. The bowl is a gift that Jim had given to her on one of their wedding anniversaries. Sometimes she will float a blossom on it, and other times it will just be the water centered on her living room coffee table. As she fills and centers the bowl each day, she takes a few moments to talk to Jim. Although she still has strong periods of sadness, her chest pain and other symptoms began to improve after this imagery journey.

ACTION STEPS

In many ways the guided imagery session is only the beginning of bringing wisdom to life. We can live it, and we have our entire life to do so, breath by breath.

The purpose of imagery is not to live from one mode of perception instead of others. Rather, imagery is an extremely valuable but underutilized resource that can be added to the spectrum of our capabilities so that we may live more fully.

For example, if a clear vision arose through imagery for a new career, the parts of us that are good at researching, planning, and taking action can support that new direction. Questions that can prompt you to take action steps include these:

- How will you begin?

- When will you begin?

- What is the first step?

- Are you willing to initiate this change?

- Are you able to initiate this change?

- What could get in the way of your following through?

- How will your life be different if you take these steps?

The imagery session may not be pointing to something as involved as a new career. If the imagery is about a relationship conflict, would it be appropriate to share your imagery journey with the person you focused on? Or if the guided imagery called up in you the desire to practice relaxation every day, can you design your schedule so that this commitment can be kept?

What can you do right now to honor your heart's wise advice?

DANIEL: HEART ATTACK

Small is the number of them that see with their own eyes,
and feel with their own hearts.

ALBERT EINSTEIN

IF HE BROUGHT an expectation of healing to our initial appointment, it was from the hurry-up-and-get-on-with-it school of life—a stoic and earnest desire for a quick solution to the recent medical distractions that had gotten in the way of significant momentum in his career in finance. Daniel had suffered a heart attack at the age of fifty-one.

In our first encounter, it was easy to see several facets of Daniel. We often think of ourselves as having a genuine, unified self. And yet the fluid nature of life evokes a broad spectrum of responses within us, and these different reactions, or selves, are layered within our personality and emerge in different situations. With Daniel, there were several distinct faces that could shift as easily as a tilt of a kaleidoscope.

When he first arrived in the office ten minutes early, he took advantage of that extra time in the waiting room to work on his laptop. His crisp, tailored appearance expressed the face of his success and professionalism. Although he seemed friendly and engaging, I think it was mostly the subtle slump in his upper back, a fatigue around his eyes, and a weight that rested in his voice that showed his face of sadness not far below the surface. And yet in certain moments, especially when he later described walks in the botanical gardens not far from his house, it was easy to see a youthful face expressing all the delight of a seven-year-old boy, eager for an adventure.

Daniel was not familiar with guided imagery, but he came on the recommendation of his physician, who prescribed imagery as a useful stress management technique during cardiac rehabilitation. In the first few sessions, we focused on some practical tools around his goals, such as reducing muscular tension by learning progressive relaxation and breathwork.

We also brainstormed some tips for ending his work focus at the end of the day in a more complete way. He was eager to do the homework from our sessions in order to meet his goals, and he did report sleeping better in the first couple of weeks.

Daniel now asks whether there is a way we could address the pain in his chest. Although the surgical procedure, which had implanted a stent in an artery to increase the blood flow to his heart, had healed well, there is still lingering pain.

Trusting the success of our work together so far, he agrees to try guided imagery and to visit his heart as a way to discover more about the pain.

"Close your eyes," I begin, "and take those long, full breaths you've been practicing."

I watch Daniel fill his abdomen with breath, then expand the breath into his rib cage, continuing until the breath rises up under his collarbones. The out-breath is just as complete, and his body softens a little more fully with each exhalation. We take time for several breath cycles to deepen his relaxation.

"Now that you are fully relaxed, bring your attention inside your chest and sense your heart. Invite an image, which may be literal or symbolic, to arise for your heart. Whatever appears, describe aloud what you become aware of."

An image arises easily, and Daniel describes his heart as "tender and bruised with blue, purple, and pink patches." He says his heart feels battered. This makes sense to him as he considers his recent surgery and heart attack. He also describes his heart as having weightiness to it, as if there is something heavy caught at the bottom. I suspect this is related to the heaviness I have heard in his voice.

I encourage him to continue exploring and ask, "If your heart had a voice, or some way of expressing itself, what would it want you to know right now?"

There is a pause, and then emotions flash across his face—eyebrows rising in surprise and then downturned lips.

He speaks with the gentle voice of his heart: "I've been waiting a long time for you to come back."

Although he can't say why he feels tearful or even knows quite what the message means, he is deeply moved and curious.

Over the next few weeks, he tells me the story of how his family had moved to this country from Eastern Europe when he was three years old. His father, who had died four years earlier, was very committed to the family and had been a hardworking man, a shopkeeper by trade. Making ends meet had not come easily in those days. When his father finally found the means to move his family to America, fueled by the strong purpose of fulfilling the dream of a better life for his children, it was a monumentous event.

With some gentle sorting out over the next several sessions, it becomes clear to Daniel that he is living his father's dream, his father's heart's desire, and not his own. He had learned early that it broke a strong family rule to voice his own view if it deviated from the family values. Although Daniel had proven to be quite capable in the business world, he had silenced his own call to landscape gardening as a young man because it did not fit the family legacy's picture of success.

"How would you like to respond to your heart's message?" I ask him during another imagery session a few weeks later.

His response arises immediately with a clear and strong voice: "I want to give my father's dream back to him so that there is more room for my own."

It's not uncommon for such a bold declaration of change to summon other "selves," other internal points of view, poised nearby. So we take time exploring his inner voices of ambivalence, guilt, and fear. He learns how to follow the banner of each of these feelings rather than ignoring them, which he had routinely done. Over time, it becomes clear to Daniel that he wants to anchor his life in the strong, clear voice of his heart that has championed his own dreams.

The intention for such deep change can be accelerated when it is made visible. This is evident in the rituals and ceremonies that arise within all cultures. They mark transitions. For example, a wedding ceremony makes visible the intention and reality of a relationship that has evolved into a life partnership. The ritual of clapping at the end of a musical performance is a ritual of appreciation and marks the transition out of the theatrical experience. I encourage Daniel to consider whether there is a way to honor his significant transition to reclaim his heart's desire through a symbol or ritual.

Not long after, Daniel arrives at our appointment and has barely taken his seat when he fishes a small round stone out of his pocket. He had found it on one of his walks at the botanical gardens in his neighborhood. He rests it in the upturned palm of his left hand.

"I'm not really a religious man," he says as he curls his fingers over the stone, "but I feel like I've been praying all week, sending thanks to my father for what he's given me. I've been imagining that the parts of my father's life I've been carrying have seeped into this stone in my pocket."

He opens his hand, showing me the stone, now infused with his father's dreams. He announces his plan to visit his father's grave next month and respectfully place the stone there.

When we conclude our work together, it is not clear whether Daniel is going to remain in the finance business or make a significant career shift. It is clear, however, that he is now making his choices, on a daily basis, more responsive to his own heart. The last time I saw him, I could recognize it in the ease of his walk and hear it through the new clarity in his voice. He had placed his fingers on the pulse of his own life and discovered the life rhythms that have heart and meaning for him.

EYES OPEN IMAGERY:
Cultivating an Awareness of Hidden Images

Throughout our lives, we have gained a lot of messages about ourselves and the world, some of which have helped us in life, and others that may have stifled us.

- Write down a belief or "rule to live by" that was expressed or implied in the family you grew up in and which may have kept you from living your life dream. Examples would be things such as, "You don't have what it takes," "Girls should grow up to be mothers, nurses, or teachers," or "The only true measure of success is wealth."

What images comes to mind with your message?

- Write about a specific time when you were influenced by that belief. Is that belief active in your life currently?

- How would your life be right now without that belief? Let that "original you," a living image, be present in this moment.

CHAPTER TEN

THREE IMAGERY SCRIPTS: DEEP RELAXATION, YOUR RADIANT SELF, RENEWED VITALITY

Now what seems to you opaque will make you transparent with your blazing heart.

RAINER MARIA RILKE

THIS BOOK IS DEVOTED to helping you find your own unique images that arise from the authentic voice of your heart. No other authority could know as much about what will truly serve you in any particular moment. Nevertheless, it can be deeply relaxing to be guided by another person, and experiencing new images can carry us to exciting inner terrain we may not yet have discovered on our own.

In this chapter you will find three such imagery journeys. The first script is designed as support for stress management and will guide you into deep relaxation. The second guided imagery, in the section "Your Whole, Radiant Self," invites you to experience your subtle, radiant "body" and to expand the sense of who you are. Borrowing from the principles of tai chi, qigong, and traditional Chinese medicine, the third script is especially beneficial in restoring vitality when you feel depleted.

There are several ways to enjoy these imagery journeys. You can record them in your own voice, setting the pace that works best for you. Read slowly with generous pauses, allowing time to deepen into relaxation. It is also a wonderful experience to share with a friend or partner, taking turns guiding each other. These scripts are also available on the website www.LeslieDavenport.com as free MP3 recordings.

Whichever method you choose, be sure to set aside twenty minutes when you can be uninterrupted by phone calls or visitors. These imagery journeys can be enjoyed either sitting up or lying down. If you find that you get drowsy, sit upright in a chair. Although you want to be comfortable and relaxed, the greatest benefits are derived from a state of calm but focused attention.

Deep Relaxation and Stress Management

There is a Zen Buddhist story that tells of two monks with a day's journey ahead of them. They are walking quietly when they come upon a river that they must cross to arrive at their destination. Near the river is a young woman, frightened of the strong current. She asks the monks if they could help her across. Although their tradition prohibits any contact with women during this pilgrimage, one of the monks quickly picks her up and transports her across the water on his back. He puts her down on the opposite bank, she expresses her gratitude, and they part ways.

As the monks continue their journey, the second monk becomes more and more preoccupied and upset as he ponders his companion's response to the woman's request. When he can no long contain his agitation, he challenges his friend. "Brother, our tradition teaches us to avoid any contact with women, but you carried her across the river!"

"Brother," the second monk replies, "I carried her for three minutes. You've been carrying her for the last three hours."

So often our experience of stress comes from the ways we carry past events with us into the present, much like the second monk who carried the distress of his companion's actions, even though the young woman was miles away. Or we generate stress by anticipation of future events, which may or may not ever come to pass. This script invites you to set down the burdens and preoccupations that you carry in order to enter a state of deep relaxation. This imagery exercise is especially effective in releasing persistent concerns that take hold of our minds. It is also useful as a transition when work is over and you are ready to enjoy your evening or in preparation for a good night's sleep.

Close your eyes.

Take a few full breaths. Be generous with your breath, drawing in oxygen that brings vitality to your body, clarity to your mind, and stability to your emotions. When you breathe out, notice that there is a letting-go quality that is a natural part of the exhalation. As you discover the letting-go feeling of the out-breath, use it to let go of muscular tension that has accumulated. Take a full body breath in, and when you breathe out, let each exhalation roll through you from head to toe. Release any sense of holding that is not needed. Let your internal organs relax as well, allowing them to feel natural and comfortable.

In the same way that you have encouraged your body to relax, let's extend the same invitation to your mind and emotions. Imagine one of those holiday snow globes that swirl with sparkly white particles when shaken. Shake one in your mind's eye, and then set it on a countertop and watch as the snowy white flecks begin to slow down and gently drift toward a resting place on the bottom of the globe. As the settling continues, feel that same quieting in your thoughts and emotions. Just let the stillness do the work. Watch the white specks come to rest and feel your thoughts and emotions coming to rest.

Now imagine that you are on a serene beach. It is a cove, open and private, beautiful and protected. The waves are very gentle, the air is fresh and pleasant, and there are patches of both sun and shade down by the water's edge. Come to a place on the shore where the dry and moist sand meet.

On the beach, take a moment to identify a situation that is distressing or confusing to you. Know that you are going to release your thoughts about this situation for a little while, returning to them later if you would like to.

Using a wooden stick, carve a word or simple picture into the wet sand to represent the stressful situation. As you write it, imagine transferring the thought from inside your mind onto the sand itself. Once you have completed drawing the word or picture, step back and look at it in the wet sand.

Now watch as the lacy edge of the sea sweeps over your concerns and begins to dissolve them. As the wave recedes, notice that your drawing is still visible but less distinct. The lines are softer. Sense the softening, your concerns dissolving.

Here comes another gentle wave, swishing over the wet sand, smoothing out your drawing even more. You can still see faint indentations from your writing but no longer a clear image. Notice that you are feeling lighter, more at ease as your thoughts dissolve in the life-affirming ocean.

And here comes one more sweep of the lovely fingers of the sea, smoothing out the sand even more, soothing your mind even more. Experience your clarity of mind now as the hands of the sea lovingly erase the last of your concerns.

Find a place on the beach to enjoy the ease in your body, your peaceful emotions, and your clear mind. Relax and be nourished by the beauty and gentle aliveness of this place.

Your Whole, Radiant Self

$E = mc^2$.

We are surrounded by light waves and sound waves. We use radio waves and microwaves. We know this through our brain waves. The invisible world, the energy realm, is in, around, and through us all the time, and it affects us profoundly.

In the medical world, energy fields are commonly used to diagnose and treat diseases. Electromagnetic fields are used in magnetic resonance imaging, radiation is used to treat cancer, and ultraviolet light is used for the treatment of skin conditions. Pulsating electromagnetic therapy has been used for the past forty years in the treatment of nonunion bone fractures. Low-power millimeter wave irradiation can enhance immune function. There's solid research demonstrating the effectiveness of high-intensity light therapy on seasonal affective disorder.

How are we assembled, what are we made of, that would respond so dramatically to such energy approaches?

Although it's been more than a hundred years since Einstein taught us that the nature of our world is energy through his famous equation $E = mc^2$, it remains a new frontier in the application and integration of this radical understanding of life.

But just because our energy-based world is now being described scientifically doesn't mean that our ancestors haven't known of it by more intuitive means. Acupuncture, which may date back to the Stone Age, describes a flow of energy, qi (pronounced "chee"), along circulatory channels in the body known as meridians. Qigong, meditation, homeopathy, and therapeutic touch are a few of the other practices with rich histories that utilize an understanding of our energetic world.

But rather than align with any particular theory, this guided imagery journey brings you into a direct exploration of your own radiant life.

Find a comfortable position to sit or recline, and close your eyes.

Bring your attention to your breath, letting it find a natural, easy rhythm. Breathe in generously; breathe out completely.

Keeping your focus on each part of the inhalation and exhalation, notice how there is a natural pause in the breath cycle following the out-breath. Feel the pause that occurs prior to the inhalation. Let the pause be a window into stillness. For the next three breaths, look through the window into the stillness at the end of the exhalation.

Now move your awareness more deeply into yourself, behind the level of physical sensations, below your emotional responses, above the activity of your thoughts. Begin to sense the pure vitality that animates your body, energizes your emotions, and ignites your mind. Feel the three-dimensional essence of your presence. Sense your energy as a kind of subtle body.

Simply breathe with this awareness of your subtle self.

In the same way that your body radiates heat beyond the surface of your skin, sense your energy body radiating beyond the outline of your body.

Notice where the energy is inside you. Feel whether it is outside. Can you find where your life source originates? Where does it stop?

As you sense and feel your energy body, let it have a color matching how you feel in this moment. Breathe that color.

Sometimes when we are intensely involved with other people and situations, we "carry" them energetically. So scan your subtle body and notice whether you sense or see other colors, other presences, embedded in your energy sphere.

If you sense another presence or color, move it to the periphery of your own energetic field using your intention and your breath. Now gently release it, letting the other color kindly return home to the person or situation where it originated. Continue with this cleansing until your energy field is completely your own. This is an opportunity to reclaim your own energy and come home to yourself.

Now sense the space beyond you. Is your energy attached to people or situations out in the world? Call yourself back home. Reel in your energy and let it blend back into your own subtle body.

When you have called your energy back to you, scan your subtle body again. Are there any holes or thin spots? Are there any dense pockets? Using your breath and awareness, smooth out your energy field, allowing any gaps to close.

Feel the glow of your essence. Be present as your subtle, radiant self. Feel your connection with the radiance of all of life.

In your vibrant aliveness, simply be home, at rest, at peace.

Vitality and Renewal

The practices of traditional Chinese medicine speak of qi, or chi, as an energy force that flows through everything that exists. Richard Gerber, a Western-trained physician, writes of a similar orientation in his book *Vibrational Medicine*.

"A system of medicine that denies or ignores its (Spirit's) existence will be incomplete because it leaves out the most fundamental quality of human existence, the spiritual dimension. . . . The tissues that compose our physical form are fed not only by oxygen, glucose, and chemical nutrients, but also by higher vibrational energies that endow the physical form with the properties of life and creative expression."

Several Eastern traditions, including Chinese and Japanese martial arts and Buddhist meditation practices, describe an energy center located in the belly, approximately three finger widths below the navel. Known as the *dantian* in China, *hara* in Japan, and *manipura* in Indian yoga philosophy, it is believed to be the reservoir of one's vitality.

This guided imagery script draws upon the practices of qi cultivation for a restorative meditation and will focus on the energy center in the belly. Although this can be done sitting or lying down, it is important to have the soles of your feet on the floor. If you are lying down, you can place a pillow beneath your knees for support.

Close your eyes.

Settle into a position where your body feels supported. Breathe in fully and evenly for three counts, setting a pace that is comfortable for you. Breathe out completely over three full counts. Continue with an even breath in, three counts, and an even breath out, three counts.

Let your breath flow into your belly, feeling it rise on the inhalation and recede on the exhalation.

As you continue breathing evenly and fully, notice the ancient rhythm within the cycle of your breath. There is a filling up and an emptying out: like the ebb and flow of the tides, the waxing and waning of the moon, the cycle of the seasons. Fill up with breath and empty out completely.

Imagine that there is a lake of energy, a vast reservoir of vitality located in your belly. Every time you breathe in, imagine that the breath brings vital energy that gets added to the lake. Picture it. Sense the depth of the lake increasing as your vitality multiplies on each in-breath. When you exhale, simply feel the presence of your life force. Breathe in, adding to your reservoir of energy; breathe out, feeling your vitality.

Now bring your focus to your eyes. Imagine and sense the very back of your eyeballs. Imagine that there is a tiny waterfall of energy that flows from the back of your eyeballs down into the lake in your belly. Let that waterfall carry any excess stimulation that has accumulated from taking in the sights of the world, and let it be recycled into the one pool of life vitality inside you. Feel the pressure from your eyes releasing; feel your eyes becoming very peaceful and relaxed.

Bring your attention to your ears, and sense and imagine your inner ears. Image all the sounds that have come to your ears also releasing like two inner waterfalls flowing down into the reservoir of your belly. Let the energy of sound release from your ears and join your inner lake of vitality. Feel your ears become quiet and peaceful as the excess energy drains into the serene pool in your belly.

Now begin to imagine a place in nature where there stands a most magnificent tree. Look at the strong trunk. Notice how the branches and leaves reach up to take in sunlight and air. Sense the tree's roots that reach down into the earth and draw up water and nutrients. Feel the tree's grand and welcoming presence.

Now come close to the tree and feel the texture of the bark; notice the rich colors. Find a way to be in direct physical contact with this beautiful tree. You may want to place the palms of your hands on its trunk or sit with your back resting against it.

Feel the soles of your feet opening to the subtle energy of the earth. Imagine that you have fine, energetic roots that reach down into the nurturing presence of the earth. Be replenished.

Tune into the contact between your body and the trunk of the tree. You have joined the natural circuitry of nutrition that flows through the tree, the earth, water, air, and sunlight. And it now flows into you, too.

Feel the generous energy of the sun, earth, water, and air. Let this natural abundance pour into you. Like a hose that fills up a swimming pool, let yourself be gradually filled with vitality as you simply rest and enjoy this beautiful place.

When you are ready, open your eyes.

Taking time in a guided imagery journey helps put us in touch with states of being that are available to us all the time. For example, when you are inside a room, realize that the air you breathe is the very same vast sky you experience outside the walls and roof. You are in the sky. You are not imagining this!

Look around and see whether there are any objects made of wood. It is the body of a magnificent tree and it still carries its organic presence. Although it has the form of a table or cabinet right now, consider its rich, natural history, and know there is sunlight and water within its grains and fiber.

There are many ways to be awake to life's mystery and gifts. Let's visit several of these traditions, assembling a personal toolbox that can enrich your guided imagery practices.

BETH: CAREER TRANSITION AND IDENTITY ISSUES

Begin challenging your own assumptions. Your
assumptions are your window on the world. Scrub them
off every once in a while, or the light won't come in.

ALAN ALDA

"I'M JUST GOING through the motions. I get in these frames of mind where I question whether I want to be a psychotherapist anymore. I can't really consider shifting careers, especially since I'm still paying off my graduate school loans. A client trusts me, and pays me to help him, and I hear a voice in my head telling him, 'Yeah, yeah—stop whining.' It's embarrassing to admit this."

Beth is giving me a look as though she's thirteen and has just smoked a cigarette behind the schoolyard. Her dark wavy hair falls over one eye, hiding her confession.

A successful, thirty-something therapist, with both a private practice and a part-time position at a community-counseling agency, Beth comes in for an imagery "tune-up" about once a month to explore whatever area of confusion is most active in her life. Today feels big, with the foundation of her career being rattled.

166

"I'm thinking if I take a certificate program in art therapy or enroll in the Jungian Institute for more training, it may revive my interest, especially if I can find a mentor. But they are both such big time and money commitments, and I don't know whether either will give me what I'm after."

I simply mirror her message back to her: "So you're hoping to discover a fresh vitality for your work as a therapist?"

The living ribbon of energy that loops between the therapist and client so often reveals the direction of the work. In hearing herself through me, Beth recognizes there is more.

"It's bigger than my career. I want to live a life with passion and depth, but I don't know how to get there. I want to believe in—in something. I want to feel the enthusiasm I see in believers. But my life feels . . . flat. I don't know. . . . I feel lost. I barely know what I'm looking for and I don't know where to find it."

Despite her apparent willingness to explore her concerns, I am aware that Beth may have to traverse some painful aspects of herself in order to connect with the passion for life she has lost touch with. Beliefs are powerful. And it is precisely her tenacious belief that she is someone lost and passionless that becomes a veil that prevents her from recognizing these qualities within.

She decides to dive into imagery and see what comes up. After some breathwork and relaxation, she enters the realm of liminal space.

"Invite an image to arise for the deep, passionate you. It may come in the form of a symbol or a felt sense. However it appears, describe aloud whatever you become aware of."

She waits and watches as a bubble slowly floats up within her and pops, revealing a figure of herself. "I'm in some kind of a barren desert. It's dusty, very dry and hot. I'm wearing something like old, olive-colored army pants and a jacket."

It strikes me that she's describing the military clothing referred to as "fatigues." As in dream work, images often have encoded messages, just as her emotional fatigue is expressed in the clothing.

"I look tired, washed out. It's not the passionate me I'm after, but I sense the passion is somewhere in this image of me. It's like I'm covered over with something, maybe it's a film of dust . . . of apathy."

I inquire if she'd be willing to explore the "covering," and she nods.

"Bring your attention to what you are sensing as the covering," I guide her, "and allow it to take shape. Let it show itself to you."

Beth is deeply engaged now, and a new image comes quickly. "I see green glass. It's that same camouflage color. There's a young girl behind the glass; it's me, about eight years old."

We pause as she takes in the whole scene. I invite her to tell me about the young girl.

"She's scared; it's not safe to come out." Beth pinches her lips and frowns with her forehead.

"It's sort of like the boy-in-the-bubble, afraid of a dangerous world."

I encourage Beth to ask this innocent little girl what she wants or needs right now.

There is a long, tearful pause, and she replies in a little-girl voice:

"She's aware of me as her adult self and she wants to tell me something. She says she can't come out from behind the glass because one of two things would happen, and they are both bad. Either she will find out that her fears are real—that the world is a dangerous, meaningless place—or she will discover that she's been wrong, that there is beauty and purpose in this world but she has wasted thirty years hardening into a shell of a person."

Naming this core belief releases a hot stream of tears. As we take time for her feelings, Beth's sobs increase as though she dropped through a chute into the caves of her sadness.

When the tears subside, I ask Beth if she would like an inner guide to join them. Beth is familiar with an imagery guide from her previous sessions. It is a comfortable way for her heart's own wisdom to join her as an image of a person, spirit, or animal.

Beth likes the possibility of a wise advisor and invites one to join her. And who appears but Carl Jung himself. He appears as a young man in his thirties, robust and enthusiastic. He greets the young girl, and she likes his company. I encourage Beth to ask if he has anything he'd like her to know.

"He's telling me to take brisk walks in the fresh air: a good constitutional every day. He's funny, but it's comforting. He has a pipe and reminds me of an uncle that I love. I don't think it's the advice itself but his undiluted confidence that feels so good to be near. He clearly believes in himself. It's that bold confidence that I want, too. We start taking a walk together, and it's as if he can transmit his confidence to me. Or maybe it's that my own confidence rises up by being close to his."

We take time for this new feeling to take hold.

"Wonderful," I comment. "Really notice what this feels like in your body, your being. . . . Where are you now?" I ask.

"Now that you ask, I realize I'm outside the glass." She laughs with surprise. "It feels good. All those intense fears of dangers and regrets were unfounded, but they seemed so true just moments ago. I hear an old voice that wants to blame me for taking so long to find this freedom, but I recognize that it would be like a butterfly blaming a caterpillar for being a slow, leaf-eating worm!" She laughs again. "It feels as though right now is the perfect moment to be right where I am. I feel the organic timing— a sense of readiness. I am a believer, and this is my true belief: to trust in the unfolding of my life, my-own-being-me-unique life, moment by moment. I can feel this is true. I have no hesitations."

We bring the session to a close, and Beth slowly opens her eyes. She looks up at me, her hair looking more like a brunette halo now as her smile shines with a brightness I have not seen in her before.

Beth came to realize that she had always been a believer. She had been a true believer in her fears, and now she is ready to believe in herself. But maybe "belief" isn't the right word for where she finds herself now. It is the direct experience of her vital spirit that she is taking into her work, her relationships, and all areas of her life. Beth decided to start each day by singing. It's her fast-track practice of plugging into her passion. By cultivating her passionate self on a daily basis, she is beginning to face confidently into the open field of her life with no glass ceilings, no glass walls.

EYES OPEN IMAGERY:

Cultivating an Awareness of Fearlessness

Have you ever spent a sleepless night worrying about a potential disaster that never happened? Or have you fidgeted nervously for a day prior to a presentation that went beautifully? We could light up a city if we converted the energy most of us expend on fearful "what if" scenarios that never come to pass.

- Answer the following questions, identifying three different desires.

  I want to ....,

  but I can't because ....

  I want to ....,

  but I can't because ....

  I want to ....,

  but I can't because ....

Some of your reasons for not pursuing what you want may have realistic restrictions: "I want to buy a house but I can't because I don't have the financial resources." Perhaps that is true, for now.

But we often block our own fulfillment with fear-based restrictions. "I want to take dance lessons, but I can't because I'm a klutz." Even if learning to dance presents a steep learning curve, labeling yourself as a klutz is a self-judgment fed by layers of fears. The fears may be a collection like these: fear of looking foolish, fear of failing, fear of being rejected. These often rest on even deeper layers of fear: if my cover is blown and others see my awkwardness, I'll be alone—forever.

Pick a fear-based statement from the exercise above, and make it into an opposite statement, listing five different reasons why you can act on your desire.

I can ....,
because ....,
....,
....,
....,
....

Using the dance lesson example given above, it could go something like this: "I *can* take dance lessons because. . . "

1. I didn't think I could ski, but I did better than I expected with the lesson.

2. When I decide I'm going to learn something, I stick with it. I'll commit to practicing.

3. I'm willing to look awkward at the beginning. I bet I won't be the only one.

4. I'll take a couple of private lessons to help me get the basics.

5. Whenever I've challenged myself, I've been glad afterward.

- Read all five answers again, letting them translate into a felt sense in your body. Feel the strength, the "yes." Let this felt sense be a living image of your fearlessness.

When there is fear, our usual instinct is to hide, fight, or run like the wind. We are programmed with this survival instinct, and it often serves us well. But as with the fears associated with the dance lessons, it is valuable to discern when we are mistaking our meek self-generated fears for a wild beast chasing us in the world.

Become very sensitive to your cues of fear. Is it butterflies in your stomach or is it the impulse to pick a fight or to start pleasing other people? Let these "symptoms" become like precious jewels. Take the time to explore the valuable message they have for you by taking them to your inner sanctuary. Let the arising of fear be a living image, a bridge to your freedom.

- Many of our chronic fears take root in childhood, and one way we can begin to heal them is by revisiting the original incident.

Think of a painful memory connected with your childhood that carries a strong message about how you should be to fit in. Maybe you were laughed at for the way you dressed or mocked for being friends with someone in a different social group or shunned for not excelling at sports. Revisit one of those moments in as much detail as possible.

Now see the young you just prior to receiving the emotional blow. See your young child's delight, curiosity, and beauty.

Let the adult you that is here right now, the one who can see this lovely child, tell her what you see. What do you want to say to this beautiful young being?

Feel the child being restored to her innocent boldness and take this precious young you into your heart. Let this feeling in your heart be a living image of your natural state of fearlessness.

CHAPTER ELEVEN

WEAVING TOGETHER IMAGERY WITH OTHER GROWTH WORK

There are many paths, and one mountain.

TAOIST PROVERB

THE MAHAYANA BUDDHIST sutra tells the story of Indra's net, an infinitely vast web suspended in the heavenly abode of the great god Indra. At the net's every crossing point is a jewel that glitters like a magnificent star. Each jewel is so completely clear that it reflects all the other jewels in the net, creating an infinite series of reflections within reflections. And because each gem is inextricably connected to all the others, a shift in one jewel means a change in all the others.

Although originally written as a metaphor for the nature of reality, the story is an apt description for the gems of self-awareness methods that mirror the inner exploration of heart-centered imagery. Approaches such as meditation, yoga, contemplative prayer, and psychotherapy each reflect a unique facet of self-exploration that can serve as a portal leading to the essence of who we are.

Guided imagery can enhance any self-awareness approach. This chapter presents three examples of blending imagery with other growth practices. Guided imagery brings the compassion of the inner sanctuary to The Work of Byron Katie, offers a way to access a high power within the twelve-step recovery model, and brings a new understanding to working with thoughts within the cognitive-behavioral method of psychotherapy.

The Work of Byron Katie

"Is it true?" This simple question is the beginning point of a powerful inquiry method that Byron Katie simply calls, The Work. *Time* magazine, which highlighted Katie in 2000 as a spiritual innovator of our times, describes her as a combination "mystical guide, wisecracking therapist, and knowing parent."

The Work of Byron Katie teaches that all suffering originates in our thinking and offers a powerful technique for questioning and freeing ourselves from the impact of our unhappy thoughts. Sometimes it's easy to identify the unhappy thought. For example, if "I'm afraid something awful will happen to my child" is the fear, then "Something awful will happen to my child" is the thought to question. Byron Katie instructs us to inquire into the stressful thought thorough four simple but powerful questions: "Is it true that something awful will happen to my child?" "Can I absolutely know that it's true?" "How do I react when I think the thought that something awful will happen to my child?" And, "How would I feel right now if I couldn't think the thought that something awful will happen to my child?" Then with a technique called the "Turnaround," we deliberately list ways the opposite of the unhappy thought could be true. This process can give us direct experiences of the ways it is our thinking, not our life circumstances, that creates our feelings of distress.

But sometimes it's hard to say what thought is causing our present unhappiness. The thought itself may be nonverbal—perhaps an impression that formed before we learned to talk. At times like these, guided imagery can give us another way to identify and transform the source of our suffering. With imagery we can start with the feeling instead of the thought. Hilda tells her story of what came out of blending guided imagery and The Work.

"I woke up feeling sad and irritable. I wasn't thinking of anything—the feelings just seemed to be there of their own accord. I also noticed that I felt a pain in my heart. I felt guilty about feeling this way when my life was basically good: I became frustrated and disappointed in myself. I started to do The Work of Byron Katie. I wrote down, 'I am sad because . . . ' I searched for the thought that the sadness was connected to, but I couldn't finish the sentence.

"I knew that this sadness has been with me on and off for a very long time, maybe my whole life, but I didn't know why. I began a guided imagery self-facilitation journey and wrote down 'my sadness.'

"I noticed that as I relaxed and traveled inward, my familiar efforts at trying to figure out my life and understand why I was sad began to release. I recognized that my thoughts had been piling on more and more levels of stress as I tried to analyze my feelings. It felt good to let go of the grip of that mental cycle. I invited an image to form for my inner sanctuary.

"I am sitting in a circle of stones on a high desert plateau. It is getting close to nightfall and the air is cooling. There is the smell of sage in the air—very purifying and fresh. The sky is a clear, deep blue with just a few streaks of white clouds. As I relax in my inner sanctuary, I imagine revisiting my topic and offer 'my sadness' for my heart's guidance.

"As I welcome my sadness into the sacred circle, my heart becomes heavier again. I hear a beautiful male voice that asks me to look into my heart. From the tone of his voice I know I can trust him and I follow his instructions. As I do so, I see in my heart a deep pool with a still, reflective surface. I look into the pool and see the faces of my parents in an argument, which was a common occurrence when I was growing up. I hear their voices saying to me, 'Fix my pain.' The image fades and then an image of my aunt, who has struggled with alcoholism, appears. She also says, 'Fix my pain.' Each time I hear that phrase, I feel a jab of pain in my heart and the weight increases. The next image that arises is my brother, the way he looked after his motorcycle accident. He turns to me with fear in his eyes and says, 'Fix my pain.'

"The weight in my heart is feeling almost unbearable, and tears are streaming down my face. The images in the pool stop now and the loving male voice speaks to me again. 'Their lives are theirs, and yours is yours. It is not possible, nor is it your job to fix their pain. Let life's mystery hold them just as life's mystery holds you. Let go of their pain.'

"I recognize the deep truth of this message. This is it—this is the thought I have believed—that I failed at my job of taking away the pain in my family. This has been the root of my sadness.

"The tears continue to flow but it feels like a releasing of the sadness now. In my imagery, the tears travel into the soil and greenery begins to spring up around me. It becomes an oasis. I feel so much lighter, and I take time resting in the peace within and around me.

"Now when the old habit of sadness returns, and it is much less often, I either revisit my heart's images, or do The Work on, 'I should have fixed their pain, is it true?'"

Using guided imagery with The Work brings loving kindness into the process from the start and surrounds you through your inquiry of your greatest nightmares. Even when you know you are ready to explore the memories and feelings of living in a war zone or financial collapse or the loss of a child, it can be daunting to face the process. Because the guided imagery journey brings you first to your inner sanctuary, you open up to your distress within an atmosphere of safety and compassion. It can be a helpful step when first approaching the experiences that have been terrorizing you for years.

Healing and Transformation through Self-Guided Imagery

Twelve-Step Programs

Twelve-step meetings occur in more than one hundred and fifty countries, and twelve-step programs have helped millions of people recover from substance abuse and addictive behaviors.

A relationship with God, or a higher power, is a core element of the Twelve-Step recovery model. From the original Twelve Steps of Alcoholics Anonymous found in *Alcoholics Anonymous—Big Book* on page 59, steps 2, 3, and 11 describe the vital role of a high power.

Step 2. Came to believe that a Power greater than ourselves could restore us to sanity.

Step 3. Made a decision to turn our will and our lives over to the care of God *as we understood Him.*

Step 11. Sought through prayer and meditation to improve our conscious contact with God *as we understood Him*, praying only for knowledge of His will for us and the power to carry that out.

Some members of the twelve-step community have an existing religious faith tradition or meditation practice that is the foundation of their relationship with a higher power, but many who come into recovery do not. God, "as we understand Him," takes many, many forms, and those forms may or may not resemble a conventional image of God.

For those twelve-steppers who are seeking to establish a relationship with a higher power, turning inward with guided imagery toward a heart-based source of wisdom and compassion can be a rich and meaningful way to discover a source of guidance greater than we know.

Juliet, a charming young woman in her mid-twenties, hit bottom when she hit the center divide of the freeway doing sixty-five miles per hour while drunk. The car accident resulted in minor injuries, a suspended driver's license, and motivation to enter recovery.

Juliet had a nine-year history of heavy alcohol use that began in high school. She was motivated to attend twelve-step meetings, but was at a loss about how to relate to a higher power. Her Catholic upbringing left her with negative impressions of a church-based faith, and she couldn't relate to the Eastern meditative practices.

Through an imagery journey, Juliet discovered a higher power that completely took her by surprise.

While doing an imagery self-facilitation worksheet, Juliet's inner sanctuary appeared as her childhood bedroom. She has many fond memories of comfort in her family home from the years prior to her rocky adolescence. It felt safe and protective in her guided imagery.

When she asked her heart for a symbol or an image of a higher power, she was puzzled by the appearance of a broken bowl. The bowl had obviously been pieced back together. After a few moments, she realized that this bowl was one that she had accidentally broken when she came home drunk late one night about eight years before. When her parents had asked about the missing bowl, she lied about it, and it had been a source of shame for quite some time. This image of a higher power wasn't making any sense to her.

But she stayed with it and asked whether the bowl had a message for her. The reply changed everything.

"You are whole, even with the cracks."

The loving response broke open the shame she had bound herself with from the patterns of addictive behavior that dominated the previous nine years of her life. She had damaged relationships with family and friends. She had damaged her school and career opportunities. She had been believing she was damaged goods.

But the bowl's message gave her a realistic hope she could relate to. She was piecing her life back together and she was essentially okay, even whole, at this point in the process.

The guided imagery process gave Juliet a reliable way to tap into a higher power. The inward process was more important than the particular symbol she received. The beautiful bowl, both fragmented and whole, may very well change over time. But for now, it has given Juliet an opening into a deep and meaningful relationship with a higher power that accompanies her in recovery.

Psychotherapy: Cognitive-Behavioral Approach

Throughout this book, we have come to see how thought patterns are responsible for perpetuating our experience of suffering. Cognitive-behavioral therapy (CBT) also recognizes the psychological impact of our negative thinking, especially thoughts that crystallize into underlying beliefs. CBT helps you change a negative thought into a positive one; guided imagery helps you change your relationship to your thinking.

There are some common ways that our beliefs distort reality, and CBT has done a great job of categorizing many of them. Notice which of the following thought patterns feel familiar to you.

Amplification, like the tempest in the teapot, is a cognitive lens that blows things out of proportion. A minor error becomes an irrevocable tragedy. An actor who forgets a line on stage believes his career is over. Procrastinating about returning a friend's call means that the other person will surely end the relationship. These habitual thought patterns constellate around a core belief, such as "I'm worthless." As each experience is interpreted through this distorted lens, it builds an arsenal of evidence that reinforces a faulty belief.

Another common thought habit is the tyranny of "shoulds." Situations become black and white, and perfectionism reigns with an ironclad list of rules about how you and others should behave. Other people may leave you feeling angry, betrayed, or confused when they violate your rules. When you break your own rules, you feel guilty and you belittle yourself.

Personalization is another way we distort reality, and when we use it, we assume that what most people say and do is a reaction to us. It is accompanied by a strong belief that we know what other people are thinking and feeling. "She smiled at me like that because she's only interested in my money." "He didn't say 'Hi' at the party because he believes what Shirley told him about me." This mind reading is rarely accurate. We end up wrestling with our own reactions to what we think is another's reaction, which may not even have occurred! Like reflections bouncing around a hall of mirrors, we get caught in a labyrinth of stressful illusions and blame others for our upset.

CBT's approach to correcting these errors in thinking is to keep a diary of the thoughts, feelings, physical symptoms, and actions that arise from a stressful situation, replacing negative thoughts and behaviors with positive ones. Adding imagery can add depth to this approach and change the fundamental relationship with thought habits.

Bruce, a gay man in his early thirties, had been working with CBT to change his experience of feeling socially awkward. His journal recorded his thoughts of being inferior to others because he often couldn't keep a conversation going. His social tension was accompanied by tightness in the pit of his stomach and a tendency to withdraw and further isolate himself. Although he practiced focusing on more realistic perspectives and new behaviors, he wasn't experiencing much improvement. He wanted to accelerate the change and tried a guided imagery journey on the phrase "I'm inferior."

Bruce's inner sanctuary was a steel vault. His shame about his social inferiority was so intense that only an impenetrable room would allow him the space to explore his distress. He could relax in the fortified safety of this most protected area, and the rare opportunity for privacy unleashed long-held tears. When he asked his heart for a response to his message, "I'm inferior," he saw an image of himself as a little boy in the Halloween costume of a clown—half yellow, half purple, with three fuzzy black buttons down the front. He remembered this as a particularly embarrassing costume his mother had picked out for him when he was ten. He sat with the image of his unhappy young self who was yearning to be free of an obligation to please his mother, and then he heard a voice that said, "You don't have to wear it."

With his heart's clear and direct message, Bruce realized he had been living by others' ideas of how he should be. In his inner sanctuary, he took off the costume, giving himself the permission to be who he is without external expectations. He didn't have to be a clown and he didn't have to be the life of the party at his social gatherings.

Ironically, as Bruce felt more at ease with his quiet nature, the natural comfort of being himself allowed him to be more socially spontaneous at times. He had both let go of his initial goal and met it anyway with changes in behavior. Guided imagery released him from the push and pull he was experiencing from attempting to resolve his issue through CBT.

You may want to experiment with recording your thoughts, feelings, and behaviors in a CBT diary and then take the juicy information, as Bruce did, to your heart's wise guidance. We have seen that what really serves us is often not accessible to our conscious minds. Going to our inner wisdom could offer a whole new direction that can only be seen with the eyes of the heart.

So whether we are questioning our thoughts, journaling our behaviors, working the twelve steps, imaging, or engaging in any other rich practices, they all point us in the same direction: being present to the miracle of life with an open heart and open mind, no matter what's going on.

Mavis: Cancer and Multiple Losses

Courage is the power to let go of the familiar.

RAYMOND LINDQUIST

PREPARED FOR A grief counseling session, I'm not expecting the spry woman with the sparkle in her eye who greets me as she enters the room. My notes from the initial phone call said that Mavis, a seventy-four-year-old woman, had recently lost her husband.

Her daughter had called in the request and provided the details, telling me that her parents had been married for fifty years. She had described a strong foundation of love that had sustained Mavis and her husband through raising four kids and finding a way through life together. In many regards, their life was a story of fairly gentle, garden-variety struggles for the first forty-five years of their marriage. But a rapid succession of painful, traumatic events has marked the last five. Mavis had been coping with breast cancer for five years and had lost her husband Fred to a brain tumor two years earlier. A hurricane had damaged their home, and she had just moved from Florida to California to live with her daughter, leaving behind her friends and church community of twenty years.

I invite Mavis to make herself comfortable and am surprised by the wiry strength beneath her slight build as she takes her seat with ease. I express my condolences: "I'm so sorry about your losses. Your daughter told me about some of what you have been through when she scheduled this appointment."

Shaking her head gently, she speaks in a lilting voice with just a hint of the South. "Oh, that sweet, worried girl of mine. I can't get her to stop fussing, but I love her to pieces. She just doesn't understand that I'm finally getting things right. Those casseroles were the last, blessed straw."

Casseroles? The non sequitur disturbs me, and I wonder whether I should assess for dementia. But she continues.

"I call it my '3 H knocks': my Health, my Husband, my House. You see, when I got cancer five years ago, I went to my familiar ways of fixing things. Planning and preparing had worked so well for so long, raising those four kids. Some part of me must have believed that if I just planned hard enough, I could hold the worst of things at bay." She chuckles a little and shakes her short gray curls. Then she tells me the sweetest story.

After she had received her cancer diagnosis, several times each week she would prepare an extra meal at suppertime, seal it in a small container, and save it in a freezer in the basement. Her plan was that when she died, her husband would be able to eat well for a long time. She saved close to six hundred casseroles, meatloaves, and stews this way, filling up four large freezers to the brim. Just when she had almost met her goal, a hurricane had knocked the power out for several days, and all the lovingly prepared meals had thawed and immediately spoiled. Then Fred became ill and died within a year of his diagnosis. Life was not going according to her plan. She turned her face toward the ceiling, but I had a sense that those milky blue eyes were seeing Florida.

"I guess my courage came to me late in this life. You see, the shock of my cancer was the first strong message that life happens out of the blue, not out of my plans.

"Taking my dear Fred, my life Sweetheart, in the blink of an eye, told me again in an even stronger voice that the fate of each day is hidden, no matter how much we want to believe that tomorrow will be pretty much like today. Plus the hurricane hit my house, the food, my plans. That was it. I just couldn't hold on anymore."

She laughs softly again, "I guess I took some pretty hard convincing. Lordy, lordy." She looks at the floor, taking a solemn moment with her memories.

The road to peace that she mostly experiences now was not an easy one. She had her generous share of sorrow, confusion, protests, sleepless nights, fear, and bargaining. She says there were times she just didn't know whether she could make it through another day with so much pain in it. She didn't think she had the strength. But she now also describes the same struggles as a journey to a remarkable freedom.

"You see, before all this happened," she explains, "I spent so much time planning my life, worrying about my decisions and how they would affect others, and wondering what would be next. I realized that if I wasn't making all those plans, I felt afraid, powerless."

She looks at me with a crooked smile. "Life showed me that I am powerless, and yet life goes on so beautifully, doesn't it?"

I wonder whether this larger-than-life woman could truly be doing so well so quickly given the multiple, severe losses she had undergone not that long ago. But I see a genuine sense of deep acceptance.

I describe the guided imagery process to Mavis, and because she does not present any therapeutic goals, I ask whether she would like to further explore her newfound freedom and way of being in the world.

Mavis agrees and leans back into the recliner. I guide her through some deep breathing and relaxation. I can see her eyes roll back beneath her eyelids, and her slowing breath indicates her readiness for the imagery. "Allow an image to form for a place that is comfortable and safe, where you can be yourself without pressures or expectations. As it takes shape, describe aloud where you are."

"I'm walking down a dirt path with lots of dry leaves along the edges. It's autumn, late afternoon—still sunny and warm, but with the faint smell of smoke and apples that tells me the cold snap is not far off. I love this time of year."

I call her attention to the range of sensory experiences to vivify the experience. "What sounds do you notice?"

"The leaves make that wonderful rustling sound as I walk, and off in the distance I can hear someone humming. Oh, I see my grandmother Rose's house. I haven't been here in . . . maybe forty years. It's so comfortable and welcoming, such a feeling of coming home. There she is on the porch in her red and white apron, and our old cat Boots is rubbing against her leg. Rose gives me a strong hug. I love being folded into her softness. I pick up Boots. His bony head rubs against my chin. My hands recognize his soft, compact body."

I find out later that both Rose and Boots have been dead for many years. With guided imagery as with dreams, the analytical mind that would ordinarily question the unusual experience becomes suspended.

"She gives me a glass of lemonade with mint leaves and tells me there is a surprise for me: Fred is waiting out back."

I can feel her excitement as Mavis describes walking along the side of the house and opening the garden gate. She tells me Fred is sitting on a wooden bench under a large shade tree. For a few, silent minutes, I receive only visual cues as to what she might be experiencing: a tender softening of her expression, a sudden raising of her eyebrows, a sharp breathy inhalation.

Although I generally ask clients to speak aloud the content of the imagery in order to best support their exploration, there is an exquisite tenderness in their encounter, and it feels appropriate for her to enjoy privacy. After a few moments, she shares aloud some of their interactions.

"As I sat down beside him, my sweet Fred gently placed a loose strand of my hair behind my ear as he did so many times over the years. I knew as he did this, that he was thanking me: he was loving me.

"I often touched him just the same way when he was in the hospital. I always wanted to hold him, touch him, but he was in so much pain, especially toward the end, that touching his hair was the gentlest way that I could.

"When he touched me just now, there was so much love in his eyes. It breaks my heart, but not in a bad way. I miss him: I have him. My heart tells me that nothing has been lost. I can feel his presence as strong as ever. Oh, my sweet Fred."

We soak together in the rich silence for a few more minutes before drawing the guided imagery to a close.

After she opens her eyes, she continues to speak tenderly about other things that Fred shared with her; how he was fine, how proud he was of her, how he is waiting for her.

But the most important part of the imagery, she tells me, was not the revisiting of the people and places from the past, nor the promise of a future reunion with Fred. She had received a powerful message.

"Yes, I do miss Fred, but our love has not diminished. Each moment includes everything if we're open to it," she says. "There's no shortage of love." Mavis leans forward in the chair, propping her elbow onto her knee, her head resting in her hand. She glances upward, searching for words.

"If I turn toward my regrets, or my anticipations, I lose life that is here right now. This moment, right now, is all we have ever had. Don't you feel it, too?"

As I sit with her, I too can feel the quiet aliveness of simply being present together. With no weight of past or future concerns, we are experiencing together an unmitigated sense of aliveness.

There are theories in the field of psychology that describe a shared field between the client and practitioner, like an energetic canvas stretching between two people painted by the words, feelings, and gestures of the therapy session. One theory even holds that certain centers in the brain begin to entrain to each other and start vibrating at the same frequency like the strings on two harps in the same room. Whatever is actually happening, there is shift from sensing the differences between two people to an awareness of a deep, unifying connection. This kind of connection felt palpable in my time with Mavis.

On the surface level, my life circumstances could not be more different than Mavis's. And yet we both know the rise and fall of expectations, of achievements and losses, of insights and relationships. And the mystery of life itself, in its awesome presence, is the essence of us both.

EYES OPEN IMAGERY:
Cultivating an Awareness of Receptivity

Most of us have a long "to do" list. Much of our time is oriented toward how to make things happen, and the quicker the better! These exercises show us ways we can also receive the gifts life offers that don't require any effort on our part. As we live with greater receptivity to the support that life provides, it creates balance in our active lives that can increase ease and decrease stress.

- Are you breathing? Or is something (life, perhaps?) breathing you? Bring your attention to your breath. Experiment with slowing it down, speeding it up, and temporarily holding it. You can influence it in these ways, but can you stop breathing?

Notice that you are actually being breathed by life, and take time to experience how each breath actually comes to you. Be aware of "receiving" each breath. Take a moment to view each breath as a living image. What is your breath expressing to you as you receive it?

- Think of a recent accomplishment and trace the origins of the achievement back. For example, if the accomplishment is, "I graduated with a master's degree," the tracing back could look like this:

  What allowed you to graduate with a master's degree?
  I graduated because I studied hard.

  What allowed you to study hard?
  I developed good work habits.

  What allowed you to have good work habits?
  My parents instilled a sense of responsibility at a young age.

  Is there an end point to the series of questions, or did it take the entire history of the universe to bring you to where you are today? What are the gifts and support that came to you along the way to your achievement?

- Write down three unexpected, enjoyable experiences you had today. They can be as simple as hearing a favorite song on the radio or a smile from a stranger, but be sure to choose experiences that came about independently of any efforts you made.

  As you experience the way life brings gifts like these to you, what does this living image of the world want you to know about who you are?

CHAPTER TWELVE

EYES OPEN IMAGERY

If the doors of perception were cleansed,
everything would be seen as it is.

WILLIAM BLAKE

WE CAN'T EXPLAIN the mystery of where we were before we were born or where we will be after we die any more than we can explain how and why we are here now. After all, we are hurtling through space on a mud ball at nineteen miles per second. I know I still have a couple of questions. What a puzzle. What a surprise. What a gift. Staying awake to the miracle of our lives rather than falling into the slumber of unhappy thoughts is the offering of imagery. To experience life fully, here and now, breath by breath, is to experience the living image of the world with the eyes of your heart.

Try this Eyes Open Imagery experiment. Look around you. Wherever you happen to be, could you let this place be your inner sanctuary? When you are at home in yourself, you are at home everywhere. Just as in your guided imagery journeys, really notice the colors, textures, sounds, and feel of the place. Know that everything you sense is comprised of the same basic substance of the entire universe—leaves, your hand, paper, light from a lamp, cement, the sky. Life is giving itself to you so richly and abundantly. Open to it. Receive it. Feel the completeness and openness of this moment. There may be things in your environment that are not your preferences, but is there anything you can see or sense that it not truly amazing in its own right? Can you find the awe in the clanging of machinery that is creating a new building, the hum of your refrigerator that keeps your food fresh, the loud voice of your neighbor who is figuring out what she needs? Give your environment, your sanctuary, a voice.

What does it want you to know right now?

One of the ways we fall asleep to our thoughts and leave the sanctuary of the present moment is when we string together three little words: *as soon as*. I will be content *as soon as* I'm financially secure, *as soon as* I'm in a good relationship, *as soon as* I'm out of a bad relationship, *as soon as* I buy a house, *as soon as* I do the laundry. We have become experts at postponing our joy to some point in the future and setting up prerequisites for our happiness. We prefer an imagined "something" we think we must have over enjoying the richness of what we do have. Anytime we leave the present moment, we leave the sanctuary of the world.

This doesn't mean that we can't make choices that lead us toward desirable life goals, but we don't need to do so at the expense of our enjoyment now. While we are overlooking the gifts of the moment, they pass and fade. Like dark pearls, we string together unhappy memories comprised of what we believe should have been different and end up wearing a garland of pain and insufficiency.

The good news is that we have the opportunity to start receiving the gifts of life right now. And I do mean right now. It's always an open invitation. As the Zen saying goes, "If not now, when?" And there is no requirement to first repent what you may have overlooked. Taking time to berate yourself is just another way to postpone your birthright of joy. The poet Jalal ad-Din Rumi reminds us that the path is always under our feet:

Come, come, whoever you are!
Wanderer, worshipper, lover of leaving.
This is not a caravan of despair.
Come. It doesn't matter if you've broken
your vows a thousand times, still
come, and yet again, come!

Young children are beautiful examples of living unconditional happiness. Whether kids have shoes or bare feet, whether they have washed behind their ears or not, they bound out of the house ready to embrace an adventure. The day is heavenly, rain or shine, and no conditions stand in the way of loving life. Perhaps it is what Jesus meant when he said, "I tell you the truth, unless you change and become like little children, you will never enter the kingdom of heaven."

Most adults, on the other hand, are ready to enjoy the day *if* (another word to watch out for) we have the right outfit, *if* it's a good hair day, *if* the right people will be there. Our minds are very creative at manufacturing a long list of requirements for happiness. We are quick to judge what's wrong with a situation at the expense of overlooking what's right, even lovely, about it.

There is an antidote for if-ing our happiness away by adding two additional letters: *as if.* I invite you to try another Eyes Open Imagery exercise. For the next twenty minutes, live *as if* life is bringing you a gift each moment, *as if* you have exactly what you need, *as if* everything you encounter is ultimately for your benefit. I'm not suggesting that you believe that these statements are true, but rather to try an experiment where you live "as if" they are true. Be like the actor who steps onto a stage, embodying a new character in an unfamiliar scene. Let the entire world that you experience be a living image of having what you need. Notice what happens as you change the lens through which you view your life.

When you're in your guided imagery inner sanctuary, it's easy to recognize your heart's guidance. But would you recognize the Buddha if he was next to you on the bus? If the guy in the next seat is in baggy jeans, a robe, or a suit, would that offer you a clue? If he smiles or is stern, would that confirm your impression? The point is not to spot a historical figure, but to discover how you can recognize the sacred by looking with fresh eyes. Are you ready to see the sacred in unexpected places and unexpected forms?

Just like a pair of trifocal glasses that bring into focus the near, middle, and distant visual ranges, the lenses of our inner perceptions are also set at varying depths. Consider this simple model of human nature.

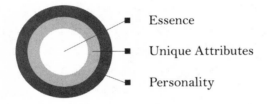

Essence

Unique Attributes

Personality

The innermost circle represents the one life force that animates us all. It is the same core essence in all of us, whatever our age, gender, social status, IQ, ethnicity, and so forth. The middle ring represents the attributes that we come into the world with. Some of us are naturally gifted at music, while others excel in math. Some people are very sensitive, and others can be relied on to take the lead in a crisis situation. The middle circle is the inherent constellation of qualities and talents that make each of us unique. The outer ring holds the roles that develop through our responsibilities. It represents our career identities; our positions as mother, daughter, and sister, father, son, and brother; our social standing; and so forth. It is the arena of our personalities in the world.

So when we meet someone new and ask, "What do you do?" we are focusing on the outer ring of the circle. This may be completely

Healing and Transformation through Self-Guided Imagery

appropriate for a first meeting at a party. But if we want to really meet life, including the person in front of us with an open heart, we also have to look more deeply. Looking into the inner circles of other people is seeing them with the eyes of your heart.

Let's first explore the midrange view within people. This is the level at which the beautiful diversity—the ways we all bring different gifts to the world—begins to show.

Just as there are no two snowflakes or fingerprints alike, everyone has a unique constellation of attributes and experiences. We don't expect a rose to have the same needs as an orchid or for a hawk to behave the same way as a pigeon, and yet when it comes to people, we often expect common values. We try to get others to relinquish their point of view, because if someone has a different opinion, surely they've just got it wrong.

Whether in marriage, friendship, communities, or nations, when differences arise, we cajole, bully, charm, argue, seduce, and threaten others in an effort to have things our way. We gain validation and comfort when others are an extension of our own viewpoints. You will hear the same refrain between many husbands and wives, races and cultures, traditionalists and liberals: "If you were just more like me, everything would be okay." And if there is a rigid attachment to the beliefs, it becomes, "My way or the highway."

The following Eyes Open Imagery practice is not about compromising around differences, but rather about fully appreciating and honoring the unique gifts we can learn to see in another.

Try this Eyes Open Imagery. Have a good friend or loved one over for coffee and try to see her as if for the very first time. See her as a living image of a unique world, unlike any other. As you are with her, be present with the respectful curiosity you would have when visiting another culture. Rather then believing that you know her based on past experience, be open to what you don't know. What have you assumed about her that may not be accurate? See her with fresh eyes.

Just as with exploring any image, notice the colors, textures, and sounds. How does it feel being with this person right in the moment? What does this "living image" want you to know? What does this person want you to know?

And now, let's explore the innermost circle of a person and learn how to focus our inner eyes on essence. As you experiment with this, it is not necessary to inform someone that you are focusing on his sacred nature. The benefit of cultivating your vision will be yours, and the world will literally transform right before your eyes. Don't be too surprised, however, if others begin to treat you differently when you see them with new eyes. States of being are contagious. Just as an agitated, angry person entering a gathering affects the atmosphere of a group, so too will you have impact on others when you are emitting an awareness of the sacredness of life.

Try this Eyes Open Imagery exercise. Take a field trip to a place where you will be around other people you don't know, perhaps a mall or a popular park. Focus your attention on the innermost essence of everyone you see. See everyone as a living image of the divine. This is not as hard as it sounds. As gently and lovingly as you can, look as gently and as lovingly as you can see. Remember that their lives arise out of the very same mystery as does yours.

Before you head out the door, let me offer you a little warning in the form of a wonderful Indian story that comes through the rich oral tradition of Hinduism. It may be useful to you when you try this Eyes Open Imagery practice.

A young man, very devoted to his spiritual life, goes to his guru for guidance. His guru tells the young man, "Know that you are God. Everything you see is also God." The young man embraces the words of his teacher and is filled with enthusiasm. He bounds down the village path thinking, "I am God. You are God. I am God. You are God."

Coming down the road heading straight for the boy is a wild bull elephant that wandered into town from a nearby jungle. A villager shouts warnings to the boy, "Get out of the way! This elephant is very dangerous."

The young man hears the warning, looks at the approaching elephant, and says to himself, "I am God. The elephant is God. Is it right to get out of the way of God?"

In a flash, the elephant charges the young man and flings him into the air with his trunk. The boy lands hard in a thorny bramble. He slowly crawls out, bruised and scraped, as the elephant runs back into the jungle.

The next day, the disheartened young man hobbles back to see his guru and tells him what happened. "You told me that I was God."

The guru responds calmly, "Yes, that is true."

"And the elephant is God."

"Quite so," replies the guru.

By now the boy is irritated. "Why, then, did I get trampled?"

"Ah!" the guru smiles. "Didn't you hear the voice of God warning you to get out of danger's way?"

Being receptive to the living images of the world is vastly different from being passive to them. If someone approaches you while you do this practice that you don't want to interact with, you can move. It's all up to you. This exercise is not about what you should or should not do. It is about focusing your inner eyes to see into the sacred heart of the world.

Well, here we are at the end of the book, but only the beginning of what's possible. We have explored together your beautiful and wise heart within and the shining heart of the world. I hope the practices have offered you assistance in finding your way to peace during distressing times. I also hope these explorations have revealed to you the obvious magnificence of who you are.

As you feel more and more at home in the fresh arising of each moment, you can receive the ever-present joy within and around you. And may your life continue to unfold in grace beyond your wildest imaginings.

RESOURCE GUIDE

COMMUNITY NETWORK

Visit www.LeslieDavenport.com and find a variety of resources to support your guided imagery practice. You can download free audio scripts that accompany the practices in this book. You can also pose questions to deepen your understanding of imagery practice. There is an online store with additional materials and CDs. Leslie's schedule is posted, and you can learn when she will be in your area.

Sign up for the free imagery newsletter and join the community of people awakening though guided imagery practice. And you are invited to send in your guided imagery journeys, adding to the rich treasury of stories of healing and transformation.

GUIDED IMAGERY TRAINING PROGRAMS

The Institute for Health & Healing

The Institute for Health & Healing at California Pacific Medical Center is the largest provider of hospital-based integrative medicine in the United States. Today, the Institute's programs serve more than 60,000 patients a year at four hospitals in the San Francisco Bay Area.

They offer a yearlong training program in integrative medicine education for practitioners to learn the application of guided imagery and expressive arts in a hospital setting with patients who have a variety of medical and surgical conditions. Leslie Davenport is on the clinical faculty and offers direct training and supervision. For more information, visit their website at www.myhealthandhealing.org, or call 415-600-HEAL.

The Academy for Guided Imagery

Martin L. Rossman, MD, a medical doctor, and David E. Bresler, PhD, a health psychologist, founded the Academy for Guided Imagery in 1989. If you are interested in becoming certified to guide others through an interactive style of guided imagery, this is an excellent training program. For information on enrolling in the Academy's professional training program, visit their website, www.academyforguidedimagery.com.

BIBLIOGRAPHY

AA Services. *Alcoholics Anonymous—Big Book* 4th edition. New York: Alchohol-ics Anonymous World Services, 2002.

Bandler, Richard, and John Grinder. *Trance-Formations: Neuro-Linguistic Programming and the Structure of Hypnosis.* Boulder, CO: Real People Press, 1981.

Bennet, John G. *Sevenfold Work.* Charles Town, WV: Claymont Communications, 1980.

Bronowski, Jacob. *The Ascent of Man.* Boston: Little, Brown and Company, 1973.

Buchanan, Mark. "Why We Are All Creatures of Habit." *New Scientist.* (July 4, 2007) 2611: p. 36.

Calaprice, Alice, and Albert Einstein. *The New Quotable Einstein.* Princeton, NJ: Princeton University Press, 2005.

Devi, Chand. *Yajurveda.* New Delhi, India: Munshiram Manoharlal, 2004.

Drohojowska-Philip, Hunter. *In Full Bloom: The Art and Life of Georgia O'Keeffe.* New York: W. W. Norton, 2005.

Eckhart, Meister. *Meister Eckhart: Selected Treatises and Sermons.* London: Far-ber & Farber Ltd, 1958.

Emmons, R. A., and M. E. McCullough. "Counting Blessings versus Burdens: Experimental Studies of Gratitude and Subjective Well-Being in Daily Life." *Journal of Personality and Social Psychology.* (2003) 84: pp. 377–89.

Ericsson, K. et al, eds. *The Cambridge Handbook of Expertise and Expert Perfor-mance.* New York: Cambridge University Press, 2006.

Esdaile, James. *Hypnosis in Medicine and Society.* New York: Institute for Research in Hypnosis, 1957.

Farrington, Tim, ed. *The Cloud of Unknowing.* San Francisco: Harper-Collins, 1981.

Gaynor, Mitchell L. *The Healing Power of Sound: Recovery from Life-Threatening Illness Using Sound, Voice, and Music.* Boston: Shambhala, 2002.

Gendlin, Eugene. *Focusing.* New York: Bantam Books, 1978.

Gerbarg, P. L., R. Brown. "Yoga: A Breath of Relief for Hurricane Katrina Refugees." *Current Psychiatry* (2005) 4: pp. 55–67.

Gerber, Richard. *Vibrational Medicine: The #1 Guide of Subtle-Energy Therapies.* Rochester, VT: Bear & Company, 2001.

Giles, Steve. *Theorizing Modernism: Essays in Critical Theory.* New York: Routlegde, 1993.

Griffiths, Bede. *The Golden String: An Autobiography.* Springfield, IL: Templegate Publishers, 1980.

Hadamard, Jacques. *The Psychology of Invention in the Mathematical Field.* New York: Dover Publications, 1954.

Hahn, Thich Nhat. *The Sun My Heart: From Mindfulness to Insight Contemplation.* Berkeley, CA: Parallax Press, 1988.

Hartmann, Franz. *Paracelsus: Life and Prophecies.* New York: Rudolph Steiner Publications, 1973.

Jung, C. G. and Joan Chodorow, ed. *Jung on Active Imagination.* Princeton, NJ: Princeton University Press, 1997.

Jung, C. G. and Gerhard Adler, ed. *C. G. Jung Letters, Vol. 1: 1960–1950.* New York: Routledge & Kegan Paul Ltd, 1973.

Jung, C. G. *Memories, Dreams, Reflections.* New York: Vintage Books, 1965.

———. *Psychology and Religion.* New Haven, CT: Yale University Press.

———. *Visions: Notes of the Seminar Given in 1930–1934.* New York: Routledge & Kegan Paul Ltd, 1998.

Katie, Byron, and Stephen Mitchell. *Loving What Is: Four Questions That Can Change Your Life.* New York: Harmony Books, 2002.

Lao Tsu. Translated by Stephen Mitchell. *Tao Te Ching.* New York: Harper and Row, 1988.

Nicklaus, Jack and Ken Bowden, contributor. *Golf My Way.* New York: Simon & Schuster, 1998.

O'Donohue, John. *Beauty: The Invisible Embrace.* New York: HarperCollins Publishers, 2004.

Oullier, O., K. J. Jantzen, F. L. Steinberg, and J. A. S. Kelso. "Neural Substrates of Real and Imagined Sensorimotor Coordination." *Cerebral Cortex*. (2004) 15: pp. 975–85.

Palmer, L. D. "The Soundtrack of Healing." *Spirituality and Health* (2005).

Picasso, Pablo, and Dore Ashton, ed. *Picasso on Art*. Cambridge, MA: Da Capo Press, 1988.

Ramsey, Boniface, ed. *John Cassian: The Conferences*. Mahwah, NJ: Paulist Press, 1997.

Ressner, J. "Four Questions to Inner Peace." *Time* (December 11, 2000) Vol. 145: p. 24.

Rohr, R. "Days without Answers in a Narrow Space—Lent." *National Catholic Reporter*. (February 1, 2002) accessed from natcath.org.

Roth, Gabrielle. *Sweat Your Prayers*. New York: Tarcher, 1998.

Rumi, Jalal Al-Din. Translated by Coleman Barks. *The Illuminated Rumi*. New York: Broadway Books, 1997.

———. *The Essential Rumi* with J. Moyne. New York: HarperOne, 1995.

Schultz, J. H., and W. Luthe. *Autogenic Training: A Psychophysiologic Approach in Psychotherapy*. New York: Grune and Stratton, 1959.

Suzuki, Shunryu. *Zen Mind, Beginner's Mind*. Boston: Shambhala, 2006.

Tagore, Rabindranath. *Stray Birds*. New York: Macmillan, 1916.

Three Initiates. *The Kybalion: A Study of the Hermetic Philosophy of Ancient Egypt and Greece*. Chigaco, IL: The Yogi Publication Society, 1940.

Tomlinson, Henry M. *Out of Soundings*. London: Beaufort Books, Inc, 1931.

Turner, Victor, and Roger Abrahams. *The Ritual Process: Structure and Anti-Structure*. Piscataway, NJ: Aldine Transaction, 1995.

Tusek, D., J. Church, S. Strong, J. Grass, and V. Fazio. "Guided Imagery: A Significant Advance in the Care of Patients Undergoing Elective Colorectal Surgery." *Diseases of the Colon and Rectum*. (February 1997) Vol. 40 (2), pp. 172–78.

Tusek D., R. E. Cwynar, and D. Cosgrove. "Effects of guided imagery on Length of Stay, Pain, and Anxiety in Cardiac Surgery Patients." *The Journal of Cardiovascular Management*. (March/April 1999) 10: pp. 22–28.

Viereck, G. S. "What Life Means to Einstein." *Saturday Evening Post* (October 26, 1929) 202: 17 p. 117.

RECOMMENDED READING

Achterberg, Jeanne. *Imagery in Healing: Shamanism and Modern Medicine*. Boston: New Sciences Library/Shambhala, 1985.

Achterberg, Jeanne, Barbara Dossey, and Leslie Kolkmeier. *Rituals of Healing: Using Imagery for Health and Wellness*. New York: Bantam Doubleday Dell, 1994.

Bolen, Jean Shinoda. *Close to the Bone: Life-Threatening Illness and the Search for Meaning*. New York: Touchstone Books, 1998.

Dikshit, Sudhakar S., ed. *I Am That: Talks with Sri Nisargadatta Maharaj*. Durham, NC: The Acorn Press, 1973.

Feuerstein, Georg. *The Yoga-Sutra of Patanjali: A New Translation and Commentary*. Rochester, VT: Inner Traditions, 1989.

Goleman, Daniel. *Social Intelligence: The New Science of Human Relationships*. New York: Bantam Books Dell, 2006.

Hanh, Thich Nhat. *Cultivating the Mind of Love: The Practice of Looking Deeply in the Mahayana Buddhist Tradition*. Berkeley, CA: Parallax Press, 1996.

Katie, Byron, and Stephen Mitchell. *A Thousand Names for Joy: Living in Harmony with the Way Things Are*. New York: Harmony Books, 2007.

Lewis, Thomas, Fari Amini, and Richard Lannon. *A General Theory of Love*. New York: Vintage Books, 2001.

Naparstek, Belleruth. *Staying Well with Guided Imagery*. New York: Warner Books, 1995.

Nepo, Mark. *The Exquisite Risk: Daring to Live an Authentic Life*. New York: Three Rivers Press, 2005.

Oyle, Irving. *The Healing Mind*. Millbrae, CA: Celestial Arts, 1987.

Pert, Candace B. *Molecules of Emotion: Why You Feel the Way You Feel*. New York: Simon & Schuster, 1999.

Remen, Rachel Naomi. *Kitchen Table Wisdom: Stories That Heal.* New York: Riverhead Books, 1997.

Rohr, Richard. *Everything Belongs: The Gift of Contemplative Prayer.* New York: Crossroads, 2003.

Rossman, Martin L. *Fighting Cancer from Within: How to Use the Power of Your Mind for Healing.* New York: Owl Books, 2003.

———. *Guided Imagery for Self-Healing.* Novato, CA: New World Library, 2000.

Samuels, Mike, and Nancy Samuels. *Seeing with the Mind's Eye.* New York: Random House, 1975.

Tolle, Eckhart. *A New Earth: Awakening to Your Life's Purpose.* New York: Penguin Group, 2005.

———. *The Power of Now: A Guide to Spiritual Enlightenment.* Novato, CA: New World Library, 1999.

INDEX

Color, infusing breath with, 88
Corpus Hermeticus, 34
Cosgrove, Dr. Delos, 33
Counting the breath exercise, 88
Current Psychiatry, 85

D

Daniel, guided imagery exercise, 7–8
"Days Without Answer in a Narrow
    Space-Lent," Rohr, 16
Devi, Chand, 36
directed imagery, 107
Dirgha Prnayama, 86–87
Diseases of the Colon and Rectum
    (journal), 33
drawing, benefits of, 144–146
dreams, describing/expressing,
    142–143
drumming, using, 92–93

E

Eckhart, Meister, 18
Einstein, Albert, 30
Emmons, Robert, 130
Emotions, identification process, 63–65
end-of-life issues, 9–13
energy centers, words for, 162
energy fields, about, 160–162
Enya, 94
Esdaile, Dr. James, 34
Evelyn, guided imagery exercise, 7
Eyes Open Imagery exercises
    about, 6, 7–8
    appreciation, 193–194
    as-if living, 191–192
    being open, 190
    being receptive, 194–195
    cultivating awareness during, 13–14,
        78–79, 102, 121–122, 155, 170–172,
        187–188

experiment, 189-190
process of, 15

F

Fazio, Dr. Victor, 33
fight-or-flight response, 81
Focusing (Gendlin), 129
Four Nobel Truths, 2

G

Gaynor, Mitchell, 95
Gendlin, Eugene, 129
Gerbarg, Patricia, 85
Gerber, Richard, 162
gifts of life, being open to receiving,
    190–191
God, nature of, 36
The Golden String (Griffiths), 19
Golf My Way (Nicklaus), 32
Graham, Douglas, 37
gratitude, benefits of expressing,
    130–131
Griffiths, Bede, 19
guided imagery process *see also* specific
    narratives
    accepting, 127–128
    acting upon, 149–150
    assumptions about, 104–109
    describing, 142–143
    overview, 1–2
    religion traditions and, 35–36
    scripts overview, 156–157
    self-facilitation guide, 47–53
    studies of, 32–33
    transitioning from, 131–132
    visualization and, 106, 109
Gurdjieff, G. I., 19–20

life vs. life conditions, 126
liminal space, described, 15–16, 18–19
Luthe, Wolfgang, 90

M

Mantras, using, 96–97
McCullough, Michael, 130
Meister Eckhart: Selected Treatises and Sermons (Eckhart), 18
Memories, Dreams, Reflections (Jung), 31
mental cause and physical effect, 34–35
mindful walking, 94
The Mirrors, 93
movement, use of, 93
music, for deep listening, 95–96
music therapy, 95
Mystic Vision: Music that Unleashes the Human Heart (Clottey), 93

N

Nadi Shodhana, 87–88
natural dance, 93–94
Ndembu tribe rituals, 15–16
"Neural Substrates of Real and Imagined Sensorimoter Coordination," 35
neuro-linguistic programming (NLP), 147
The New Quotable Einstein, 46
New Scientist magazine, 140
Nicklaus, Jack, 31–32
nose and mouth breathing, 86
nothingness, exploring, 112–113

O

O'Donohue, John, 3
O'Keeffe, Georgia, 144–145
Olatunji, Babatunde, 93
Om, about, 96
Out of Soundings (Tomlinson), 17

P

Paint the Sky with Stars (Enya), 94
Paracelsus: Life and Prophecies (Hartmann), 33–34
Pascual-Leone, Alvaro, 32
Psychology and Religion (Jung), 70
Pentland, Alex, 140
perfectionism, 179
personalization, 180–181
Picasso on Art (Ashton, ed.), 143
Planet Drum (Hart, Mickey), 93
Psychology of Invention in the Mathematical Field, The (Hadamard), 30
psychoneuroimmunology, 34

Q

qi cultivation exercise, 162–165

R

Rabindranath Tagore, 6–7
re-identification, mental habits and, 124–125
receptive imagery, 108, 129
relaxation practice
  overview, 83–84
  autogenic training, 90–91
  progressive relaxation, 89–91
  The Skylike Mind, 92
  stress management, 157–159
  thought-based, 91–92
  The Witness, 91–92
relaxation response, creating/ maintaining, 81–83
Rilke, Ranier Maria, 156
Ritual, benefits of, 148–149
The Ritual Process: Structure and Anti-Structure (Turner), 15–16
Rohr, Richard, 16

ABOUT THE AUTHOR

Leslie Davenport is a pioneer in the role of guided imagery in psychotherapy and integrative medicine. She is a licensed marriage and family therapist, with master's degrees in the arts and psychology, and she is an ordained minister in an interfaith Sufi tradition. Leslie was a founder of the Humanities Program at Marin General Hospital, which evolved into the Institute for Health & Healing in collaboration with California Pacific Medical Center in San Francisco. Leslie has more than ten years' teaching experience at universities, including Mills College, University of San Francisco, California State University Hayward, and Holy Names University, and she served as core faculty with the Transpersonal Psychology Graduate Program at John F. Kennedy University.

Leslie is currently in practice in Kentfield, California, and at the Institute for Health & Healing at California Pacific Medical Center in San Francisco. She is also on the clinical faculty with the Institute for Health & Healing's Integrative Medicine Certificate Program. The author of numerous articles in the field of integrative medicine, she served as editorial consultant to Aspen Publishers for their book, *Promotion and Complementary Therapies: A Resource for Integrative Practice*. She was honored in her home county with the Marin Breast Cancer Council's Honor Thy Healer award. Her work continues to be influential in a health-care revolution that recognizes the role of meaning and the spiritual dimensions of life as an integral part of health and healing.